# Chevrolets
## *of the* *1950s*

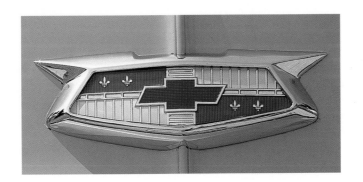

# Chevrolets
## *of the* 1950s

**Tony Beadle**

Motorbooks International
Publishers & Wholesalers ®

*This book is dedicated to my father, W.W. "Bill" Beadle, for instilling in me a love of that glorious contraption, equipped with an internal-combustion engine and wheels, that we call the automobile.*

This edition first published in 1997 by
Motorbooks International Publishers & Wholesalers,
729 Prospect Avenue, PO Box 1, Osceola, WI 54020 USA

© Windrow & Greene 1997

Previously published by Windrow & Greene Ltd, London

Library of Congress Cataloging-in-Publication Data Available.

ISBN  0-7603-0395-9

Printed and bound in Hong Kong

*Front cover* **In 1954, the Bel Air was the top of the Chevrolet line-up, having its own distinctive body trim that contained the Bel Air name and Chevy crest on the rear fender. The '54 models were the last to be offered with a six-cylinder engine only - the light and powerful V8 was on its way.**

*Back cover* **Clockwise, from top left: 1951 Series 3600 pick-up truck; 1952 DeLuxe Styleline two-door sedan; 1950 DeLuxe Fleetline four-door sedan; 1954 Bel Air two-door convertible and 1954 Series 3100 pick-up truck; 1955 Bel Air two-door sedan; 1958 Impala two-door sport coupe; 1957 Bel Air two-door convertible; 1959 Impala two-door sport coupe; 1956 Bel Air two-door sport coupe; 1953 Corvette.**

*Page 1* **The Chevrolet emblem, seen on more new cars than any other brand during the 1950s.**

*Page 2* **Chevy light trucks were as stylish as the cars.**

*Opposite* **Chevrolet sales throughout the 1950s helped them lay claim to the title "heartbeat of America".**

# CONTENTS

# AMERICA'S NUMBER ONE

When they launched their 1954 models, Chevrolet used the slogan: "Year After Year, More People Buy Chevrolets Than Any Other Car." For most of the 1950s, this was true, not just corporate publicity hype. And, on the rare occasions when they lost the number-one spot to arch-rivals Ford, Chevy always ran a close second.

In the decade covered by this book, Chevrolet averaged an output of approximately 1.3 million automobiles per year. But it wasn't only cars: light-duty pick-ups, trucks and panel vans bearing the Chevy bow-tie emblem also streamed off the production lines, accounting for at least another third of a million new vehicles each year during the 1950s.

In total, the 1950s saw more than 16 million new Chevrolet cars and trucks flow onto the highways of America, a glittering river of steel and chrome, 17 vehicles wide, that would stretch all the way from New York to California! No wonder Chevrolet subsequently claimed the title of "America's Heartbeat".

**The 1950 Chevrolet was not regarded as a particularly hot performer in its day, but rather was seen as a rugged and reliable means of daily transport for Ma and Pa America and their family. It is very similar to the 1949 Chevy, the two vertical bars in the lower part of the grille providing an instant means of identification.**

Not that Chevy had always ruled the roost so emphatically. They only took the number-one spot in 1927 and 1928 when Ford shut down production for six months to switch to making the new Model A, after churning out Tin Lizzies for 19 years. Ford was back on top in '29 and '30, but Chevrolet regained the lead in 1931, and from then on, the two giants slugged it out for the top spot, with Chevy taking the honors more often than not until 1942. On their 23rd birthday - November 3, 1934 - the company celebrated the production of ten million units.

Car production came to a halt when the USA entered World War 2, following the Japanese attack at Pearl Harbor on December 7, 1941. (Some auto manufacturers had been producing armaments for Britain, Russia and China under the lend-lease programme for over six months by then.) The last pre-war Chevy came off the assembly line on February 6, 1942. During the war, Chevrolet factories built aircraft engines, amphibious

*Above* **It was cars like this 1931 Independence three-window coupe that enabled Chevrolet to dominate arch-rivals Ford for most years during the 1930s and early 1940s, before civilian vehicle production was halted by the United States' entry into World War 2.**

vehicles, guns, armor-piercing shells and particularly trucks - thousands upon thousands of them - that saw action in every corner of the world.

Even before the formal Japanese surrender on September 2, 1945, Detroit's attention had shifted back to civilian automobiles, the US government having swiftly canceled military contracts when the outcome of the conflict was no longer in doubt. The first post-war Chevrolet was built on October 3, 1945, in Kansas City, and a total of 12,776 cars were delivered to an eager public before the end of the year. Undoubtedly, it would have been more had it not been for a strike by 325,000

*Above* **This 1938 Chevy Master DeLuxe four-door sedan is typical of the staid styling used by the company in the latter part of the decade. Even so, and despite the more streamlined looks of the Ford models, Chevrolet kept ahead in the sales race.**

*Below* **By 1940, Chevrolet front-end styling had evolved somewhat, with headlights now mounted on top of the fenders. Compared to that year's Fords, the styling still lagged behind a little, but sales forged ahead as Chevy again took the number-one spot by a wide margin.**

General Motors workers, which began on November 21 and lasted for 119 days.

Like the cars offered by every other US manufacturer at the end of 1945, these "new" Chevrolets were identical to the 1942 models produced for the few months before the country went to war. Identical, that is, apart from a few minor alterations to the front grille and trim. It didn't matter: after three years of being unable to buy any new cars, and with dollars to spend, the public was hungry for product: it was a seller's market. Almost anything with an engine and wheels was snapped up.

Chevrolet really got into their stride in 1946, turning

out 397,109 automobiles and 270,140 trucks. In the process, they reclaimed the number-one spot that Ford had occupied for the few short months that made up the '45 model year. Once again, these '46 offerings were merely updated '42 models, employing ageing body styles and the inline "Stovebolt" six-cylinder engine that dated back as far as the 1929 model year. On the car front, this situation was to remain for the 1947 and 1948 model years, although numbers sold continued to increase dramatically as Mr and Mrs America aspired to a new car sitting in the driveway. On December 5, 1946, Chev-rolet's 19 millionth vehicle was produced.

While Chevrolet car design remained static immediately after the war, events were taking place at the top of the company that were to affect the marque's future. In June 1946, M.E. Coyle was replaced as general manager by Nick Dreystadt, formerly of Cadillac, who forcefully encouraged development of new designs and engineering changes. Unfortunately, Dreystadt died suddenly two years later, and his successor, W.E. Armstrong, was forced to resign shortly after taking over because of ill health. Thomas H. Keating then assumed control and, following the initiative laid down by Dreystadt, promoted Chevrolet's entry into the 1950s with gusto.

Chevrolet's trucks received the first complete redesign

*Above* **Easily the person who wielded the most influence over automotive styling in the 1950s was Harley Earl, the enigmatic head of General Motors' Styling Division, seen here behind the wheel of the 1951 Buick LeSabre concept car. The jet aircraft influences in the design are immediately apparent, but the LeSabre had many other advanced features for its day, including an electrically adjustable driver's seat and a powered convertible top that would be raised automatically if it began to rain!**

*Left* **This 1942 Chevy half-ton pick-up is a prime example of the type of truck churned out by the thousand during**

World War 2. "The Jacksonville Flyer", as it's dubbed, is painted in the gray livery of the US Navy. This style of light-duty pick-up first appeared in 1941 and remained in production until Chevrolet's Advance-Design range of commercial vehicles appeared in May 1947.

*Right* The 1946 Chevrolets, such as this Fleetmaster four-door sport sedan, were little more than 1942 models with minor alterations. Even so, due to pent-up demand for new cars caused by the war, buyers snapped up everything the auto manufacturers could produce. Four-door models were the top selling Chevys in '46.

*Above* **A Chevrolet Fleetmaster convertible was used as the pace car for the 1948 Indianapolis 500-mile race, which was held on May 31 and won by Mauri Rose at an average speed of 119.814mph.**

*Below* **The Fleetline two-door Aero Sedan was far and away the most popular Chevrolet in 1948, 211,861 being sold. That was the peak for the fastback body style, however, and it was dropped after 1952. The only differences between a '47 and a '48 model Chevy were the vertical T-shaped bar added to the grille, a new hood ornament and a slightly revised badge. Describing the Aero Sedan as ultra-distinctive, the brochure went on to say: "...marks a new high in the art of body designing. It closely approaches the ideal in streamlining, yet makes no sacrifice of roominess and comfort."**

of the post-war years in 1947. Unlike cars, trucks continued to be built throughout the war, enabling the company to plan ahead for the introduction of new civilian models. The Advance-Design range of pick-ups and vans went into production on May 1, 1947, after Chevrolet had interviewed truck owners and operators across the USA. Top priority, the survey revealed, was a larger, roomier cab for the driver, with better visibility and greater comfort. Chevrolet also believed that styling would play an important role in truck choice - a good looking vehicle brought added prestige to its owner's business - but understood that any changes in appearance could not be at the expense of practicality or economic operating costs. So successful was the Advance-Design concept that Chevy trucks remained much the same until 1955.

The 20 millionth Chevrolet rolled off the line on November 13, 1947, at the new Flint, Michigan assembly plant. Only nine months later, on August 30, 1948, the 21 million mark was passed.

The following year was a milestone for the American auto industry, as over six million vehicles poured from the assembly plants, more than the entire combined production from the rest of the world. Of much greater significance for Chevrolet, however, was that 1949

# CHEVROLET *Advance-Design* TRUCKS

*Above* **Chevrolet trucks were the first to be given a new post-war look (the cars weren't redesigned until 1949) with the launch of the Advance-Design range of vehicles in May 1947. Concentrating on driver comfort and attractive styling, without compromising load carrying capability or economy, the Advance-Design proved such a success that Chevy trucks remained virtually unchanged until 1955.**

marked the introduction of their first really new passenger-car designs since the end of the war. Masterminding the bold styling strokes that were to mark the opening of one of the most memorable decades in American automotive history was the legendary Harley Earl. Head of General Motors' Styling Division, and a vice-president of the corporation since 1940, Earl was in a unique position to shape the look of the American automobile throughout the 1950s, and other manufacturers wasted no time in following his lead.

Harley Earl's main influences came from aviation. He used jet and rocket themes extensively in his car designs, but undoubtedly his most famous contribution was the tailfin, a styling feature that subsequently found its way onto the cars of every nation, in one form or another. In 1945, according to GM president Alfred P. Sloan: "We concluded that the consumer would rank styling first, automatic transmission second, and high-compression engines third." Now, at the beginning of the 1950s, they were getting ready to offer all three, even on the cheapest Chevrolet model.

Behind Harley Earl were the combined talents of the Chevrolet design studio, initially headed by Ed Glowacke and, after April 1951, by Clare "Mac" MacKichan.

NEW CHEVROLET for 1950

*Smarter Styling · New Luxuries · Improved Performance*

*Above* **This sales brochure proclaimed that Chevrolets were new for 1950, but in fact, styling had changed little from the previous year.**

*Below* **In 1953, the Corvette was born. Although in its initial unsophisticated form, the two-seater almost failed to survive, with the arrival of the V8 engine, it became a true high-performance machine. This 1953 'Vette shows off its low-slung, rounded profile, set off by the distinct belt-line trim linking front and rear bumpers, and protruding taillights mounted in rocket-like housings.**

There was also the invaluable help of Chevrolet's energetic and forward looking chief engineer, Ed Cole, who took over the post in May 1952 from the more traditionally-minded Edward H. "Crankshaft" Kelley. It was Kelley who had been responsible for the design of the crankshaft for the Stovebolt six engine (hence the nickname), and for him the inline-six *was* Chevrolet. Ed Cole realized the need for a new V8 to compete in the horsepower race of the mid-1950s, and he was instrumental in creating the fabulous "small-block" Chevy V8 engine, which first appeared in 1955 models as a lightweight 265cu.in. (4.34-liter) powerplant producing 162bhp.

The real boom year for Chevrolet was 1950, when they became the first company to manufacture more than two million vehicles in 12 months: a rate of over 12 vehicles a minute. At the beginning of the decade, 15 plants in 11 different cities made up the Chevrolet manufacturing organization, and during 1950, three produc-

tion marks were realized: on January 11, the 23 million total was passed; 24 million came up on June 30; and 25 million on December 22. Quite a year!

In 1950, the full force of what became known as "planned obsolescence", or the annual complete design change, hadn't quite taken hold, so in that year, Chevrolets looked much the same as they did in '49. The same was true for '51, but from then on, the pace quickened. Shortage of essential materials, such as steel, chrome and nickel, resulting from the United States' entanglement in the Korean war, slowed things down for the first three months of 1951, when car and truck production was cut back by the National Production Authority (NPA), under the state of emergency declared by President Truman. However, once the brakes were off, things really began to move.

During June 1953, in a small area to one side of a factory in Flint, Michigan, hand-built, fiberglass-bodied sports cars began to appear at the rate of just three a day. These were the humble beginnings of the Chevrolet Corvette. Another Harley Earl brainchild, the two-seater was far from an instant success: only 300 were made as '53 models. Although styled in the manner of European sports cars, the newcomer lacked their performance and handling capabilities. As a result, the axe nearly fell on the Corvette before it became properly established, but the persistence shown by Earl and Ed Cole paid off when the new V8 became available, and another piece of American folklore came into being.

*Below* **The big breakthrough in the early 1950s was the introduction of automatic transmission in low-priced automobiles. Chevrolet offered its two-speed Powerglide as a $159 option in 1950 DeLuxe models, and it was an instant winner. This 1952 brochure praises the automatic "For low-cost motoring at its smooth and easy best."**

*For low-cost motoring at its smooth and easy best*

POWER*glide**

1953 CHEVROLET

*Entirely NEW through and through!*

Corvette apart, the years 1952 to 1954 were a time of transition for Chevrolet; in those days, the lead time for new car designs could be as long as three years, so the foundations for the '52-'54 models had been laid well in advance. But the revolution was to come with the introduction of the 1955 models. Working under the celebrated Harley Earl edict, "Go all the way, then back off," Clare Mackichan, Chuck Stebbins, Bob Veryzer, Carl Renner and the rest of the Chevy design team created an undisputed classic automobile, powered by a supreme V8 engine.

*Above* **According to the copywriters, 1953 Chevrolets were "Entirely NEW through and through!" However, while the exterior looked good, with its one-piece, windshield, heavy chrome grille, and so on, underneath was the same old six-cylinder Stovebolt engine.**

*Below* **The 1955 Chevy Bel Air models came like this two-door coupe - sporty looking, with an attractive two-tone paint scheme - and thanks to the new V8, their performance matched that appearance.**

General Motors did celebrate one significant event in 1954: the production of its 50 millionth automobile. This was a gold 1955 Chevrolet Bel Air sport coupe, which was paraded around the streets of Flint in a motorcade. In the meantime, Chevrolet was busy clocking up its own marks of 29, 30 and 31 million.

The US auto industry enjoyed a bonanza year in 1955. To a record total of eight million cars built, Chevrolet contributed 1.8 million. The numbers dropped a little in

*Above* **On November 23, 1954, a gold painted Chevrolet Bel Air two-door hardtop came to the end of the assembly line in Flint, Michigan. It was the 50 millionth vehicle to be built by General Motors, and the "GOLDEN CARnival" celebrations included a parade through the city, and a 15-minute slot on national television as part of the Chevy sponsored Dinah Shore show. GM president Harlow M. Curtice was interviewed on the TV program, which also featured a cavalcade of Chevrolets from the earliest models to the new offerings for 1955.**

'56 and '57, and although today these Chevrolet model years are often regarded as totally separate entities, in fact, they were heavy facelifts on the basic '55 design. That doesn't prevent them from being appreciated for the great cars they are, however, and for whatever reasons, the 1957 Chevrolet has become forever enshrined as *the* American car of the 1950s.

Redesigned Chevrolet "Task Force" trucks were also unveiled in 1955, featuring more sculptured lines and many technical improvements that were to help keep the company ahead in the sales race for light-duty pick-ups and vans. In addition, the change of appearance and greater comfort saw the genesis of the light truck as a leisure vehicle. No longer were Chevy pick-ups only bought by farmers and contractors as utilitarian work-horses: now they appealed to a whole new class of buyer, who viewed them as dual-purpose vehicles that could be fun and practical, yet acceptable just about anywhere. From now on, Chevy trucks were to be restyled every year, just like the cars, but the basic Task Force structure lasted until 1959.

This period also saw Chevrolet move away from its traditional low-price slot in the General Motors pecking order. Top-of-the-line Chevy models now had many luxury accessories as standard, and they competed in the medium-price bracket, while the "stripped" cheap cars, with the bare minimum of equipment, attracted fewer customers. It was an age of selling more car per unit: more luxury, more accessories, more powerful engines - with continual improvements and innovations. The more glamorous (and more expensive) body styles, such as hardtops, convertibles and station wagons, became increasingly popular.

The slump came in '58. As Chevrolet models grew larger and rounder, sales dropped by nearly 40 percent, hit by a recession in the US economy. Sales of smaller, economical imported cars were growing dramatically; of the US makes, only Rambler, with its compact American

*Below* **Restyling for 1956 was limited to a facelift of the '55 models. The most noticeable change to the front end was the use of a full-width grille and square parking lights. This Bel Air hardtop displays the curiously shaped side trim that was only used on '56 models.**

*Above right* **The quintessential American classic of the 1950s: the 1957 Chevrolet. This was the third and last year for the two-door Nomad sport wagon, although the four-door Nomad continued to the end of the decade and beyond. The '57 Chevy is so familiar that it hardly seems necessary to point out its salient features: the oval bumper and grille, the twin windsplitz in the hood, air intakes above the headlights, sharp tailfins and sweeping aluminum rear fender trim panels. They provide an unmistakeable image. The model sold like hot cakes, and remains sought after today.**

*Right* **Chevys became larger, fatter and rounder for 1958, and sales dropped as the US economy hit a bad patch. The Bel Air (such as this four-door sedan) was no longer regarded as the most luxurious model in the Chevy line-up, following the introduction of the new Impala coupe and convertible.**

*Above* The Corvette was restyled for '56 and remained little changed in '57. New front fenders, chrome-rimmed headlights, a sweeping cove along each side of the body, and taillights set into the rear fenders produced a design classic. Not only did the looks improve, but also the performance to match, thanks to the new V8 engine.

*Below* In 1959, Chevrolet launched the El Camino, a stylish pick-up based on the passenger-car platform as a somewhat belated answer to Ford's Ranchero, first introduced in 1957. Although several publicity photos emphasized the El Camino's suitability as a working truck, this shot promotes it as a dual-purpose vehicle that could be driven almost anywhere. In purely practical terms, the huge sprawling tailfins, futuristic double-curvature rear window and roof overhang were superfluous features, but don't they look great?

model, showed any gains over the previous year. Only comparatively recently have 1958 Chevrolets, like the Impala that made its debut that year, begun to be looked at more favorably by serious collectors.

As the end of the decade approached, things were set to change. Harley Earl retired in December, 1959, to be replaced by William Mitchell as head of design. For the 1960s, fins were shorn and much of the glitz removed.

In 1959, the El Camino made its debut. This car-based pick-up was intended to take advantage of the new leisure-vehicle market. Full-sized Chevy cars grew ever larger (although for '59 and '60, vertical tailfins were replaced by horizontal gullwings), as a sizeable number of the buying public still felt that "bigger was better".

Chevrolet ended the 1950s on top, although not by much. There can be little doubt that the policy formulated by General Motors, as far back as 1921, of offering "a car for every purse and purpose" had paid dividends. In the early 1960s, GM president John Gordon said: "Taking into account all of the colors available and all of the optional equipment we now offer - power assists, air conditioning, tilt steering wheels, autronic eyes and so on - we could, in theory at least, go through a whole year's production without making any two cars alike.

*Above* **This 1957 Cameo Model 3124 pick-up is a typical example of the Task Force design of Chevrolet light-duty trucks, which ran from 1955 to 1959. A revised grille and a greater choice of optional colors were the main alterations from the previous two years, but this '57 is in one of the two standard colors, Cardinal Red (the other was Bombay White). The "V" emblem on the door signifies that the truck is equipped with a V8 engine.**

Our objective is not only a car for every purpose but, you might say, a car for every purse, purpose and person."

Never can there have been such a colorful and exciting decade for the American driver as the 1950s; nor, it seems, is there ever likely to be again. As America's number one, Chevrolet, perhaps more than any other make, reflects perfectly an age of chrome, two-tone paint and wraparound windshields - a time when a high-speed nation got behind the wheels of land-based rocket ships and headed down the uncrowded highways, in search of a bright new tomorrow.

Chevrolet's theme tune, used in television commercials throughout the 1950s, was a catchy little number that ran: "See the USA in a Chevrolet!" - many millions of Americans did just that.

# 1950

## FIRST AND FINEST AT LOWEST PRICE

Chevrolet began the 1950s with cars that were basically mild updates of the designs that had been introduced for the 1949 model year. The '49s represented the first all-new Chevy body styles for seven years, as the immediate post-war offerings had been no more than 1942 models with different front grille and trim treatments.

The new Chevys had a shorter wheelbase, reduced by an inch to 115in, but thanks to a lower roof height (down by 2.5in) they managed to look sleeker than before. Front and rear tread widths were also reduced slightly. Although the chassis was of similar rectangular box-section construction as previously, the revised front suspension had its shock absorbers mounted inside the coil springs for the first time, and while the same worm-and-roller-sector steering box was used, the steering linkage itself was modified. Wheels remained at 15in diameter, but now had five-stud fixings. The new slab-sided body styles featured front fenders that swept back into the doors, more streamlined rear fenders, and curved, two-piece windshields to give a clean and rounded appearance. Visibility was improved by a 30

**Almost identical to Chevrolet's first all-new, post-war car design, introduced in 1949, the 1950 DeLuxe Fleetline four-door sedan displays the beginnings of 1950s styling exuberance.**

percent increase in glass area, which also contributed to the overall illusion of a longer, lower profile.

For identification purposes, the most obvious difference between the '49 and '50 Chevrolets was to be found in the front grille. On the earlier cars, the lower section of the grille had seven vertical bars; later models had only two. Also, the '50 trunk handle was fixed, and the lid opened by simply turning the key, whereas the '49 handle had to be turned as well. Otherwise, the two model years were virtually identical.

The Chevrolet line-up for 1950 consisted of two series - Special and DeLuxe - with convertible and station

*Below* **Higher-priced DeLuxe models had chrome body and window trim that was not found on cheaper Special line cars. Bumper extensions, or wings, were options.**

wagon models only available in the higher-priced DeLuxe series. The rest of the range consisted of two- and four-door sedans (given the Styleline name to define the bustle, or notch-back, design), and a couple of two-door coupes, with the utilitarian business coupe built for traveling salesmen and commercial use as part of the base Special series. Fleetline models, with their long, tapering rear roofline, came in two- and four-door sedan versions, as either Special or DeLuxe types.

Introduced to Chevy dealers in January 1950, the automobiles that were to put the company at the top of the yearly sales chart yet again could be regarded as a mixture of old and new. Names destined to become part of the American way of life, like Bel Air and Powerglide, made their debut, while the sweeping fastback of the Fleetline was to disappear in a couple of years. The two-

door hardtop Bel Air model undoubtedly pointed the way forward, and this body style, giving the illusion of a steel-roofed convertible, proved extremely popular throughout the 1950s. Likewise, the two-speed Powerglide automatic transmission ($159 extra on DeLuxe models only), which shared some similarities with the Buick Dynaflow, was to be a mainstay of Chevrolet for many years to come. In addition, the tried and trusted Stovebolt six-cylinder engine now had hydraulic lifters, which got rid of most of the familiar valvetrain clatter experienced on earlier Chevy sixes.

The continued use of an inline-six, while the rest of the industry were looking at V8 engines, should, in theory, have weighed against Chevrolet, but such was the Stovebolt's reputation for reliability and durability that Chevy sales topped the 1.5 million mark for the first time. In fact, the overhead-valve Stovebolt engine had been a Chevrolet fixture since the 1929 models, although it had been updated regularly. Cars equipped with the new Powerglide automatic had a bigger 235cu.in (3.85-liter) version, a development of the truck engine introduced in 1941. This had larger-diameter inlet valves, a larger bore and longer stroke, and it generated 105hp, against 90hp from the 216.5cu.in (3.54-liter) engine fitted to cars with the manual transmission.

By no stretch of the imagination could the 1950 Chevrolet be described as a hot performer, but the reputation earned in previous years of providing value for money in the low-priced bracket stood the company in good stead. Top speed was in excess of 85mph, but acceleration to 60mph from rest took 19 seconds. Neither figure would be likely to raise the heart rate a great deal these days, but they were more than adequate for the time. Chevy adverts pushed the "valve-in-head" engine design, as all their rivals were still using flatheads, and tried to promote its performance potential with such lines as: "Step out in a Chevrolet and enjoy

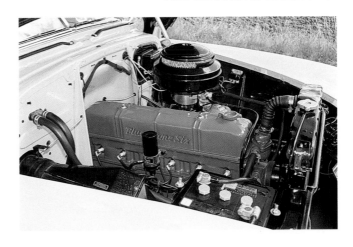

*Above* **Cars with the Powerglide transmission were fitted with the 235cu.in Blue Flame six-cylinder engine and a lower (3.55:1) rear axle ratio.**

*Above* **In the main, a single Rochester carburetor was used, but Stromberg and Carter carbs were also fitted.**

*Above* **Bench seats provide seating for six. Dark and light gray interior colours were standard on all 1950 Chevrolets, but patterns differed from model to model.**

25

higher thrills with lower costs every minute, month and mile you drive!" Other features pushed in Chevy advertising included: "Center-Point Steering and the Unitized Knee-Action Ride for maximum steering-ease and riding-ease", and "Curved Windshield with Panoramic Visibility and Proved Certi-Safe Hydraulic Brakes for greater safety protection."

One other Chevy carry-over from 1949 was the all-steel-bodied station wagon, a model that had been pioneered by Plymouth, closely followed by Oldsmobile and Pontiac. The woody had been around since the beginning of the automobile, but in the 1950s, it was finally laid to rest, although the use of wood-effect decoration on station wagons continued for many years.

The top selling Chevy in 1950 was the DeLuxe Styleline four-door sedan, which accounted for almost a quarter of the 1.3 million cars of that model year produced by the company. Options available for the DeLuxe range included a pushbutton radio, a heater and defroster, a radio antenna, fog lamps, an external sun visor, whitewall tires and a locking gas filler cap. There was a host of other items, too, many of them installed by dealers rather than the factory.

Assembled at the Baltimore, Maryland plant, the DeLuxe Fleetline shown here was one of the first Powerglide equipped cars to be produced and, as a consequence, was kept for a year by a GM factory director for evaluation purposes before being sold on.

In view of what was to come later in the decade, and with hindsight, the styling of those 1950 Chevrolets could be regarded as fairly conservative. This is not surprising, given that the cars were aimed first and foremost at Mr and Mrs Average. The transformation of Chevrolet from a manufacturer of sedate, low-priced family automobiles to a purveyor of lively, high-performance machines was under way, albeit falteringly, but it would be a few years before the change was complete.

*Top* **From the side, the Fleetline sedan has a smooth, flowing look. Note the DeLuxe script just behind the front wheel opening, above the body molding, and also the chrome stone guards at front and rear. The chrome cover for the fuel filler flap is a period accessory.**

*Above left* **Without power steering, a large-diameter steering wheel is essential. The knob on the rim helps handle sharp corners and tight parking situations. With**

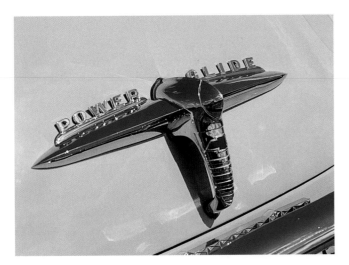

dual interior visors, an exterior sun visor would seem almost unnecessary, but it looks great! The gadget mounted on top of the dash is a prism for viewing overhead stop lights.

*Above right* **The fixed rear trunk lid handle is a distinguishing feature of 1950 models. The "Powerglide" logo proclaims that this Chevy is equipped with a two-speed automatic - a first in low-priced automobiles.**

## 1950 CHEVROLET DELUXE FLEETLINE FOUR-DOOR SEDAN

### Engine
OHV, inline six cylinder, cast-iron block and head
Capacity: 235cu.in (3.85 liters)
Bore and stroke: 3.56x3.94in
Compression ratio: 6.7:1
Power output: 105hp at 3,600rpm
Torque: 198lb/ft at 1,650rpm
Carburetor: Single Rochester one-barrel

### Transmission
Powerglide two-speed automatic

### Chassis/body
Wheelbase: 115in
Overall length: 197in
Shipping weight: 3,145lb
Suspension: Coil spring independent front; semi-elliptic leaf springs with semi-floating rear axle
Wheel diameter: 15in

### Performance
Top speed: 87mph
0-60mph: 19.35sec
Standing quarter mile: 21.05sec at 63mph

### General
Factory price, 1950: $1,529
Production total: 124,287

# 1951
## ADVANCE-DESIGN

On the commercial transport front, Chevrolet had long held an enviable position as America's leading supplier of trucks and vans. As far back as 1933, half the yearly output of new vehicles for business, industry and agriculture bore the Chevy bow-tie emblem. And for only one year between the end of World War 2 and 1959 did Chevrolet fail to dominate the US truck market.

As with their cars, immediately post-war, Chevy offered trucks that were, for the most part, the same as pre-war examples, with one or two engineering refinements. However, on May 1, 1947, Chevrolet Advance-Design trucks began to come off the assembly lines. With their stylish good looks, they heralded the start of a process that eventually would lead to the hitherto strictly utilitarian pick-ups and vans being seen in a new light - as leisure vehicles.

With the introduction of the Advance-Design, Chevrolet took the opportunity to separate its truck models into two groups. Smaller pick-ups and vans were given the name "Thriftmaster"; "Loadmaster" was used for larger trucks. While the styling remained basically

**This Advance-Design Series 3600 pick-up sports many optional extras, such as the chrome grille, bumpers and side mirrors. It has an extra strengthening brace fitted to the side of the cargo bed, in front of the rear fender.**

*Above* **As befits a working vehicle, the interior of the pick-up cab is pretty sparse and features a simple dash layout. The parking brake is foot operated and positioned on the left, with a T-handle release mounted under the dash.**

*Above* **Tower of chrome? This unusual angle makes the truck grille seem like a construction of mammoth proportions. The rectangular parking lights are tucked away at the top and outer ends of the grille, adjacent to the headlights.**

the same for both groups, changes obviously had to be made to cope with the physically larger dimensions of the cabs and bodies in the Loadmaster category. For the purposes of this book, we are only considering light-duty pick-ups, as they form an integral part of today's collector and enthusiast vehicle market.

Diverting from trucks for an instant, let's take a brief look at Chevrolet automobiles in 1951. These were facelifted versions of the 1950 models and, again, only a couple of minor changes were made to the grille and body trim. Sales dropped slightly to 1.25 million, due in part to government restrictions aimed at conserving steel and other strategic materials for the Korean war effort, but also because the sellers' market was beginning to contract. However, Chevy remained as the nation's number-one auto maker.

Although 1951 was the fifth year for the Advance-Design, that year's Thriftmaster pick-up truck looked much the same as one built in '47. Outside, there were very few changes, but under that curved new skin, mechanical development continued as part of an ongoing improvement process.

Compared to the '46 and earlier trucks, the body was wider, offering an extra 8in of hip room for the driver and passenger. In fact, the cab interior dimensions were increased in almost every direction to provide a more spacious environment. The wider, deeper windshield was raked at a greater angle and fixed so that the wipers could be mounted at the bottom. Ventilation was provided by a cowl top vent and an opening flap just in front of the driver's door, but the introduction of vent windows in '51 saw this side flap disappear. The hood sloped slightly down toward the radiator and was hinged at the back, providing easier access to the engine. The headlights were fully incorporated into the squarer fenders, while heavy horizontal grille bars gave the front a modern look for the 1950s.

Advance-Design pick-ups were identified by their load carrying capacity: Series 3100 for half-ton and Series 3600 for three-quarter ton. On '49 and later trucks, these series numbers were located on each side of the hood, to the rear, below the Chevrolet name badge. The wheelbase for the Series 3100 was 116in, and 125.25in for 3600 versions, but the chassis of both had the same overall dimensions. The chassis were reportedly of stronger construction than the earlier trucks. The suspension was based on leaf springs front and rear, with a semi floating rear axle in the 3600, and a fully floating axle for the 3100 series. Hydraulic brakes were fitted to all four wheels, and for '51, these were uprated to give greater efficiency. The rear bumper was made optional that year to allow the tailgate to drop to the fully vertical

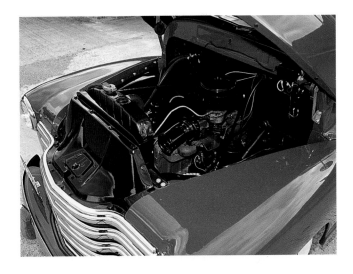

*Above* **The Advance-Design hood, which opens from the front, makes the six-cylinder engine more accessible than in earlier trucks.**

*Below* **Chevrolet described the turret-top cab as having "observation car vision", thanks to increased glass area.**

## 1951 CHEVROLET THRIFTMASTER SERIES 3600 PICK-UP TRUCK

**Engine:**
Inline, six cylinder, cast-iron block and head
Capacity: 216.5cu.in (3.54 liters)
Bore and stroke: 3.50x3.75in
Compression ratio: 6.6:1
Power output: 92hp at 3,400rpm
Torque: 176lb/ft at 1,600rpm
Carburetor: Single Rochester one-barrel

**Transmission:**
Three-speed manual

**Chassis/body:**
Wheelbase: 125.25in
Overall length: 206in
Shipping weight: 3,470lb
Suspension: Leaf springs front and rear; I-beam front axle and semi-floating rear axle
Wheel diameter: 15in

**General:**
Factory price, 1951: $1,508
Production total: 271,017*

* Production total is for all pick-ups and trucks up to 1-ton models; separate figures are not available for 3600 series

*Above* **Wide whitewall tires look good on this Series 3600 pick-up, but were unlikely to have been fitted by the factory in '51. The row of 11 small louvers on the cowl shows that this truck has a factory fitted heater. In the same position on the other side of the cab is a vent that directs fresh air to the driver.**

position for easier loading. This entailed relocating or revising the rear lights, exhaust, spare wheel carrier and license plate.

Under the hood was the tried and tested Stovebolt six, which produced 92hp from 216.5cu.in. Like the similar-sized car engines, the truck powerplant had mechanical valve lifters. A three-speed manual transmission was standard and could be specified with either a floor or column mounted gear shift; the optional four-speed came with a floor shift only. Many other options were made

*Above* **In 1951, Chevrolet automobiles, such as this DeLuxe Styleline convertible, showed few changes from the preceding model year. The front was altered slightly by moving the parking lights into the lower grille, below the headlights, with five vertical bars alongside. The Chevrolet name in the top grille frame was written in** **script, rather than block letters. Only DeLuxe models had the stainless steel side spear, which stepped up over the front wheel opening, and the chrome rear fender gravel shields; lower priced Special models had plain body sides. The engine/transmission specifications were the same as for 1950 models.**

available over the years, ranging from Nu-Vue quarter windows, which improved rearward vision, to extra chrome trim.

In adverts aimed directly at the farming community, Chevy promoted their trucks as offering all-round value, and stated: "...whatever the hauling job - here are trucks made with a mind to working comfort and convenience, power and economy!" And there can be no questioning the durability of the Advance-Design trucks. Even today, especially in the dry states, such as California and Arizona, you can find unrestored examples in regular daily use, still working for their keep.

Finally, a confession. The immaculate truck shown in this chapter actually isn't a 1951 model at all - it's vintage 1950! By way of explanation, it must be said that there is so little difference between the trucks of the Advance-Design era (1947-53) that it would take a rare expertise and close scrutiny to identify them. Barring a few tiny details, the vehicle shown has the exact specification and overall appearance of a 1951 model.

# 1952

## BLUE FLAME STYLELINE

In some respects, this year could be regarded as a minor watershed in Chevrolet's history. Up to, and including, the 1952 models, the influences of pre-war design were still clearly evident. Henceforth, however, the school of 1950s styling was to come into its own, bringing with it all the glitz and glamor for which the period is remembered.

Changes were afoot elsewhere in American society in 1952: the Truman presidency came to an end, and Dwight D. Eisenhower was elected to the White House, following a campaign directed against the Korean war, Communism and government corruption. Ike's pledge to go to Korea if he won was seen as a good vote catcher, and subsequently, in July 1953, the three-year conflict came to an end.

Material shortages due to the Korean war effort became apparent in a variety of ways. Whitewall tires were in short supply, as were precious nickel and other metals. As a result, the original factory chrome plating of the period wasn't always as good as it should have been. (In the case of the car featured here, the central

**Although a genuine 1952 model, this Chevy has the plain central grille bar of the '51 cars, possibly because of material shortages during the Korean war. This was also the final year for split windshields on all Chevrolets.**

horizontal bar in the front grille - a genuine original fitment - is that of a '51 model, not the normal '52 version with five pressed "teeth" in it. Whether this oddity was due to shortages caused by the war, a surplus of old parts, or a lack of new components isn't clear.) Defense contracts awarded to Chevrolet caused some cutbacks in car production so that the government orders could be fulfilled, but expansion of production facilities went ahead with the construction of 2,000,000sq.ft of new plant buildings.

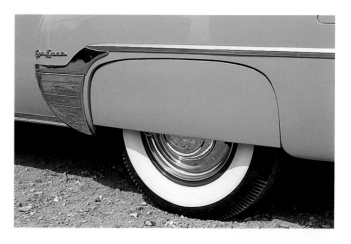

This was to be the last year for the Styleline and Fleetline names, and the only fastback car in the Chevrolet line-up for '52 was the Fleetline two-door sedan. In every respect, the Chevy was a conventional automobile, as one would expect from a company whose top selling model was a four-door sedan, designed for the average American family with 2.4 children. The familiar inline six-cylinder engine, three-speed manual transmission with column shifter, coil-spring-and-wishbone independent front suspension, leaf-spring rear suspension and live rear axle could not be regarded as pushing the envelope of automotive technology, even in the early 1950s.

But that familiarity was undoubtedly one of the reasons for Chevrolet's continued success. While the Powerglide automatic transmission, introduced in 1950 models, proved extremely popular (the millionth Powerglide equipped Chevy to come off the line was assembled in October 1952), there were still plenty of customers who opted for the more traditional methods of driving. That attitude was changing, however, and the pace of change was increasing. It would continue to do so throughout the rest of the decade.

For the automotive journalist in 1952, it was difficult to pinpoint precisely why Chevrolet sold more cars than anyone else. Walt Woron, of *Motor Trend*, carried out a two-car comparison test (one manual, the other with

*Above left* **Fender skirts were only fitted on DeLuxe models. Whitewall tires might have been difficult to find in 1952, but there's no such problem today.**

*Below left* **The badge on the hood was new for '52. The top grille bar, with Chevrolet name, is another leftover from the 1951 model, but has been on this car since new.**

*Right* **Taillights changed very little in the period 1950-52; "blue dots" are period custom accessories.**

*Below* **The body side trim on the front fender and door is a single plain strip, very similar to that of 1950 models, but positioned lower, like 1951 models. The bright metal stone guard on the rear fender was only used on the DeLuxe series; cheaper Special versions had a rubber guard and no fender skirt. A distinguishing feature of '52 Chevys is the extra trim piece running from the top of the stone guard back across the rear fender.**

*Above* **The simplicity of the Chevrolet powerplant can easily be seen here; regular maintenance is no problem in such an uncluttered engine bay.**

*Above* **The DeLuxe dash with central chrome "waterfall", a recurring Chevrolet feature during the early 1950s.**

*Above* **Gray cloth upholstery was used extensively by Chevrolet in '52, but the combination of patterns and shades on door panels varied from model to model.**

automatic transmission) and commented: "What makes the Chevrolet a good car? It's somewhat hard to pick one outstanding feature, but its best feature is its handling...both of the test cars cornered flat, did not hop, or give any indication of front end mushiness."

Woron also thought that the steering was accurate, but needed a fair amount of driver effort, adding: "There is no wind wander and a pleasant absence of road shock through the steering wheel." The ride was regarded as being on the firm side, but met with overall approval, as it gave a feeling of "big car solidity..."

From a safety point of view, driver vision got the thumbs up, but the brakes rated less highly. Even though he could apparently find no trace of fading after repeated heavy brake tests, Woron considered that they could still be improved because "...at medium to high speeds considerable pedal pressure is required."

On the performance front, the manual-transmission car proved quicker on acceleration, reaching 60mph in 20.46sec and going on to achieve a top speed of 83mph. Woron commented dryly: "Neither of the two Chevys has any rubber burning tendencies." In that respect, the Chevrolet lost out to rival Ford which, with its V8 powerplant, could post significantly better numbers. But, as the Chevy executives knew full well, speed and acceleration were yet to be major selling points - when they became important factors, Chevrolet would be ready. Probably more significant was the Stovebolt's reputation for reliability and ruggedness, together with its simplicity and ease of maintenance - that sense of familiarity again. An average fuel economy figure of 20mpg didn't do any harm either.

As far as the Chevy six engine was concerned, there were two versions in '52: manual-transmission cars had a 92hp, 216.5cu.in unit, while for Powerglide equipped models, a 102hp, 235cu.in variant was used. The latter had a slighter larger bore and longer stroke to compensate for the extra power required to drive the automatic transmission.

A hint of what was to come could be found with the increasing appeal of the Chevy Bel Air hardtop design, which took over from the fastback style as the sporty element in the Chevrolet range. Otherwise, 1952 remained a typical year from the early part of the decade, styling varying only slightly, with minor details like grille, taillights and body trim being altered, while prices remained competitive.

Chevrolet kept the usual two separate model groups

*Below* **The extra bar attached to the top of the bumper guards is not a standard factory fitting, while the "blue dots" in the rear lights are nostalgia custom items. Although they have a certain period charm, they would seldom have been seen on a new car in '52.**

### 1952 CHEVROLET DELUXE STYLELINE TWO-DOOR SEDAN

**Engine:**
OHV, Inline six cylinder, cast-iron block and head
Capacity: 216.5cu.in (3.54 liters)
Bore and stroke: 3.50x3.75in
Compression ratio: 6.6:1
Power output: 92hp at 3,400rpm
Carburetor: Single Rochester one-barrel

**Transmission:**
Three-speed manual

**Chassis/body:**
Wheelbase: 115in
Overall length: 197.75in
Overall width: 74in
Shipping weight: 3,110lb
Suspension: Coil-spring independent front; semi-elliptic leaf springs with live rear axle
Wheel diameter: 15in

**Performance:**
Top speed: 83mph
0-60mph: 20.46sec

**General:**
Factory price, 1952: $1,696
Production total: 215,417

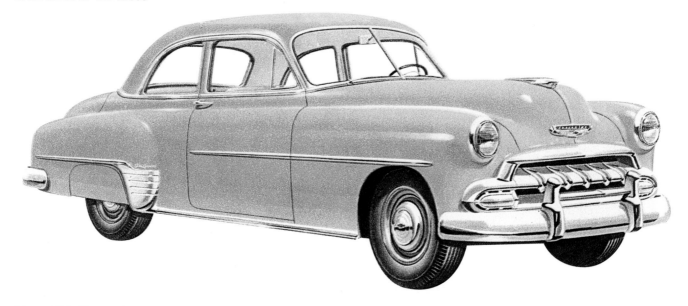

*Above* This illustration was taken from Chevrolet's 1952 catalog and shows a DeLuxe Styleline two-door sedan; compare it to the genuine article featured on the preceding pages.

*Below* This factory publicity shot of a DeLuxe Styleline convertible coupe shows some evidence of retouching. Black sidewall tires were fitted, as whitewalls were in short supply. In total, 11,975 convertibles were made.

for '52, named Special and DeLuxe, the cheaper Special models being outsold at the rate of more than six to one by the expensive cars. Given that the price difference could be as much as $600, when the top selling Special Styleline two-door sedan cost just over $1,600, this represented a tremendous surge in demand for more luxurious looking automobiles - even at the very bottom end of the market. Special models had no chrome body trim, rubber rear fender stone guards and open rear wheel openings, but were available in a choice of nine single exterior colors and four two-tone combinations. Prices ranged from $1,519 for the bare-essentials two-door business coupe to $1,659 for a four-door sedan.

By way of contrast, the DeLuxe Styleline range had plenty of bright metalwork to set off its extra selection of body colors, plus fender skirts and much more glitz on the dash. Prices started nearly $50 above the top Special model, and went to almost $2,300 for the four-door station wagon. In other words, largely superficial or cosmetic "dress-up" items were used to create the notion of an upmarket car worth all those extra hard earned bucks. It might have been only a Chevy in the driveway, but it was a DeLuxe Chevy, and it looked as good as almost any other new car on the road.

Chevrolet brochures described the 1952 range as: "America's most beautiful low-priced car." While that statement may be regarded as typical publicity hype, there was no disputing the company's success in the marketplace.

*America's most beautiful low-priced car*

**CHEVROLET**

*Above* **This sales brochure illustration clearly shows the '52 grille design with its five "teeth" on the middle bar. Compare this to the photograph on pages 34 and 35.**

# 1953

## CORVETTE: DREAMS ON WHEELS

There can be no denying that the creation of America's favorite sports car was almost entirely due to the enthusiasm and determination of two men: Harley Earl and Ed Cole. As a vice president of General Motors, designer Earl was in a uniquely powerful position, and undoubtedly it was through his influence that the Corvette became a reality. Cole, Chevrolet's chief engineer, also saw the sports car as a way of boosting the company's traditional image as a producer of staid sedans for the average family man.

Alongside these two, the names of Robert McLean and Maurice Olley should also be added. Then a young man, fresh from Cal Tech, McLean took an unconventional approach to achieving a 50/50 weight distribution when laying out the chassis: he started at the rear axle and worked forward. Olley, an ex-Rolls Royce engineer who had joined GM in 1930, took care of most of the chassis, suspension and steering details. Their work helped Earl give the Corvette its essential ground hug-

**This side view of a 1953 Corvette reveals how much of an afterthought the top was! This particular car received a Bloomington Gold Certificate from the National Corvette Certification Board on the basis that its overall originality and condition were judged to be within 95-100 percent of what they were on the day it left the factory.**

*Above* **The first Corvette is driven from the production line in Flint, Michigan, by Tony Kleiber, a body assembler. Standing behind are R.G. Ford (left), manager of Chevrolet assembly plants, and F.J. Fessenden, Flint assembly plant manager.**

*Below* **The Blue Flame engine was uprated to 150hp, but still lacked the necessary performance image. The metal shroud over the distributor and spark plug leads prevents radio interference in the fiberglass-bodied car.**

ging sports car stance, which was aided by positioning the engine and drivetrain arrangement quite a bit lower than the norm.

In the past, much has been made of the fact that interest in sports cars, during the early 1950s, was due to young military personnel returning from Europe with MGs and similar cars in tow. What is rarely mentioned is just how few of these small two-seaters were actually on the road. In 1952, only 11,000 sports cars were registered in the entire USA, representing a tiny 0.025 percent of all new cars registered. Therefore, it's not surprising that the big Detroit manufacturers were not over anxious about missing out on such an apparently minuscule sector of the market.

But Harley Earl was nothing if not a dedicated car enthusiast and, having developed a strong affection for the likes of Jaguar and Ferrari, he wanted to prove that GM could build something that was as good, or even better. At the time, fiberglass was receiving a lot of

attention as a possible alternative to steel for car bodies, and it seems that Earl manipulated this interest as a means of putting together a prototype in time for the GM Motorama - a glamorous cavalcade of exotic dream cars that toured the country every year between 1949 and 1961. Demand for the new Corvette was immediate and feverish, Chevrolet dealers fielding innumerable enquiries concerning delivery and price of the sporty looking two-seater, but most of these potential customers were destined to be disappointed.

The first of the 300 Corvettes produced as '53 models came off the end of a short, six-car-long assembly line in a corner of the Flint, Michigan factory on June 30. They were virtually handmade, the 46-piece body being supplied by the Molded Fiber Glass Body Co of Ashtabula, Ohio, and the chassis by another outside supplier. The engines were shipped in from the Chevrolet plant in Tonawanda, New York. Sometimes, manufacture was a rather fitful process. It had been

*Above* **Having struggled to put the original top up and free it of wrinkles, the owner of this car wasn't about to put it down again just for a few photographs! This Minnesota car is number 43 of the 300 produced in the first year.**

*Below* **Triple Carter YH sidedraft one-barrel carburetors, on a special aluminum manifold, are part of the tuning package developed by Ed Cole and his engineers to boost the output of the ancient 235cu.in Stovebolt six.**

decided that these first examples would only be sold to prominent personalities, and cars were strictly allocated. However, this policy was to rebound when initial demand failed to live up to expectations. In part, this was due to problems with the cars themselves, creating unhelpful publicity from the various celebrities who had been chosen as customers. Another hindrance was the price: at $3,490, the Corvette was over $1,000 more expensive than an MG, and well beyond the reach of the young buyers for whom it had been conceived originally. The fact that the car was a Chevrolet didn't help either - that traditional image of dull reliability was a definite stumbling block.

Chevrolet's general manager, Thomas Keating, said at the time: "In the Corvette we have built a sports car in the American tradition. It is not a racing car in the accepted sense that a European sports car is a race car. It is intended rather to satisfy the American public's conception of beauty, comfort and convenience, plus performance."

Unfortunately for Keating and Chevrolet, comparisons between the Corvette and European sports cars were inevitable, and for dyed-in-the-wool enthusiasts, the Chevy was found wanting in several respects. The two-speed Powerglide automatic, the dashboard layout and whitewall tires were not seen as belonging on a true "sports car". And although Jaguar also employed a six-cylinder engine, it was of an exotic overhead-camshaft design, not a revamped Chevy truck motor. Even those drivers who were prepared to overlook the Corvette's performance shortcomings found plenty to complain about when it came to "comfort and convenience", including crude clip-in side curtains instead of wind-up

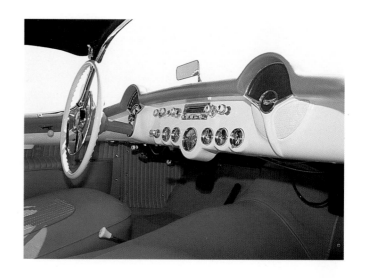

*Right* **Another view of the convertible top shows how much it restricts rearward and sideways vision. Note the fuel filler flap positioned right behind the driver's door.**

*Left* **The dashboard styling is almost perfectly symmetrical. The large dial in the center is the tachometer, which is flanked by auxiliary gauges. The passenger-side cowl matches the speedometer and houses the radio speaker. A Sportsman Red interior was standard on all 1953 Corvettes.**

*Right* **Another unusual feature of early Corvettes are the two interior knobs for opening the doors - there are no exterior handles.**

windows, a primitive folding top that limited vision, dust and water leaks, and body rattle.

To be fair to the designers and engineers at Chevrolet, a lot of the components used in the Corvette were chosen because they were already available from the parts bins, which helped reduce both costs and development time - important considerations in this type of limited-production project, but certain to result in compromises. Some were unavoidable, like the engine. In 1953, the only choice at Chevrolet was the inline-six, but Ed Cole and his crew coaxed 150hp out of the old Stovebolt. They fitted a hotter camshaft with higher lift and longer duration, solid instead of hydraulic lifters, stronger valve springs, three Carter YH sidedraft carbs on an aluminum manifold, and a modified cylinder head with the compression ratio raised to 8.0:1. It all added up to a top speed approaching 110mph.

Other changes were required to fit the engine under

the low-profile hood. The water pump was moved down so that the fan blades had sufficient clearance, while the front portion of the valve cover was rounded off for the same reason.

With the transmission, Chevy engineers were also in a fix. The standard three-speed manual gearbox just wasn't up to the job, and buying one from a specialist supplier was deemed too expensive, so almost by default, the Powerglide automatic became the choice. Perhaps Harley Earl thought the automatic would appeal to drivers of a more sybaritic nature than those whom the Corvette would supposedly attract; if so, it was a misjudgment. The luxury lovers demanded more than the Corvette was equipped to give, even if they only intended to use it on sunny weekends and brought out the family Buick or Cadillac sedan for daily driving. On the other side of the coin, the automatic was derided by the high-performance sports car brigade, so the

*Above far left* **With twin chrome exhaust stubs protruding through the body and mini fins on rocket-like taillights, there can be little doubt as to the aeronautical influences on Harley Earl's design of the rear end.**

*Above left* **The stainless steel mesh headlight stone guards were removed in some states, as they did not conform to local vehicle laws. Some magazine writers expressed concern about possible body damage when parking due to the lack of full bumpers, each corner of the body being equipped with a "bumperette".**

*Above* **Although 6.70x15in U.S. Royal wide whitewall tires were listed as an optional extra, the factory usually fitted them anyway. Chevrolet identification is provided by a badge in the center of each hubcap, and the name in script on the body. The sleek styling of the convertible Corvette masked quite a few teething problems, particularly in getting the 46 separate fiberglass body components to fit together and cure properly.**

## 1953 CHEVROLET CORVETTE

**Engine:**
OHV, inline six cylinder, cast-iron block and head
Capacity: 235cu.in (3.86 liters)
Bore and stroke: 3.56x3.94in
Compression ratio: 8.0:1
Power output: 150hp at 4,200rpm
Torque: 223lb/ft at 2,400rpm
Carburetors: Three Carter YH one-barrel sidedraft

**Transmission:**
Powerglide two-speed automatic with floor shift

**Chassis/body:**
Wheelbase: 102in
Overall length: 167in
Overall width: 72in
Shipping weight: 2,705lb
Suspension: Coil-spring independent front; leaf-spring rear with live axle
Wheel diameter: 15in

**Performance:**
Top speed: 107mph
0-60mph: 11.0sec
Standing quarter mile: 18.0sec at 76mph

**General:**
Factory price, 1953: $3,498
Production total: 300

*Above* **Like the headlight guards, the clear plastic cover over the inset license plate was not legal in some states.**
*Below* **The main proportion of 1953 Chevrolet car production comprised four-door sedans, like this Bel Air, which has been fitted with extra front bumper guards. The price for the four-door model was $1,874, and nearly a quarter of a million were sold.**

Corvette ended up by pleasing few people. Unless, that is, you count some of the journalists who wrote magazine road test reports.

Hank Gamble was almost lyrical in the June 1954 issue of *Motor Life*: "To sum it up, the Chevrolet Corvette is a true sports car, offering the prospective buyer tops in performance. It has a few 'bugs' as does any model first or last, but none are so extreme as to discredit the car to any degree. The Corvette is a beauty - and it goes!" *Road & Track*, of August 1953, praised "excellent workmanship and attention to detail" in the fiberglass body, and went on: "The fabric top is much better in appearance than most imported cars and folds into a flush compartment behind the bucket type seats." But it's no accident that almost all official factory pictures show the car with the top down!

Only 183 Corvettes were sold in 1953, and in 1954,

production had to be restricted after the manufacturing operation was moved to St Louis. The Corvette was almost killed off. However, with the arrival of the new V8 engine, it was destined not merely to survive, but to become one of America's automotive legends.

On the "bread and butter" side, meanwhile, Chevrolet were still leading the field, selling over 1.3 million of their heavily revamped 1953 models. Gone were the Fleetline and Styleline names, as the fastback models were deleted from the line-up. Instead, Chevrolet offered three series: Special 150, DeLuxe 210 and Bel Air. The four top-of-the-line Bel Air models featured the most chrome trim, luxury fittings and extras such as rear fender skirts. With the exception of club coupes, convertibles and station wagons, all '53 Chevy models had a large wraparound rear window, while power steering became available for the first time as a $178 extra.

*Above* **From the very first to the present day, crossed Chevrolet and checkered flags have been used as the Corvette emblem.**

*Below* **Kansas City, Missouri, June 9, 1953. Another milestone is reached as the 29 millionth Chevrolet, a Bel Air two-door sport coupe, makes its way to the end of the production line**

# 1954

## FINE AND THRIFTY, SOLID AND STEADY

Although America had been a nation on the move for several decades, thanks to mass production of the automobile, 1954 was a time of tremendous expansion in road building. The US government had announced a huge ten-year program that was projected to cost $50 billion. While much emphasis would be placed on the construction of a network of interstate and intercity highways, there was also provision for improving local "farm-to-market" routes.

And it's a fair bet that whether traveling swiftly and smoothly on one of the new super highways, or bouncing slowly along an old country dirt road, you would see more new Chevrolet cars and trucks than any other make. In 1954, however, this was by only the slimmest of margins. The race for the number-one sales spot was almost too close to call, as arch rivals Ford launched an intense sales campaign, offering their cars at "less than cost" and gaining an increase in model year sales. Chevrolet countered by pushing more cars out to the

**This Bel Air convertible and half-ton pick-up truck illustrate perfectly the style of vehicles offered by Chevrolet in 1954. Over 40 years on, the workhorse truck has achieved a glamor and collectible status that, although not quite on a par with the ragtop, could not have been foreseen when it was new.**

*Above* **The Chevy bow-tie emblem on the hood was of a smaller design in '54, while the ornament displays the aeronautical influences that were in vogue at the time.**
*Below* **There is ample room for five people in the convertible. Note the split back on the front bench seat, allowing passengers easy access to the back seat.**

dealers and pumped their calendar year figures above the competition. At least one magazine referred to the 1954 Chevrolet as "the best selling car on earth."

As the previous year had seen a major restyling of Chevrolet passenger cars, there were no startling alterations for '54, just minor design revisions and small technical improvements. The new grille and heavier bumpers gave the cars a more aggressive look, and although the wheelbase stayed at 115in, those bigger bumpers increased the overall length by almost an inch. Engine modifications included a higher-lift camshaft, aluminum pistons instead of cast iron, a more rigid crankshaft and an increase in oil pressure from 35 to 45lb/sq.in. There were two versions of the 235.5cu.in six: 125hp when fitted with the Powerglide automatic, and 115hp with the three-speed manual transmission.

In his road test of a Powerglide equipped Bel Air four-door sedan, published in the April '54 issue of *Motor Life*, Griff Borgeson enthused about the improvements

in performance: "...a stimulating car to drive" and "...a machine capable of cruising all day in the 80s" were just two of his comments. But he was equally impressed by the car's looks: "...the beautiful Bel Air convertible offers an almost unbeatable combination of luxury, looks and selling price." Borgeson went on to note how such luxury items as power seat adjustment, and power assisted windows, steering and brakes were all available as options, at a price that practically any car owner could afford. His final statement confirmed the perceived status of the company as America's number one: "Chevrolet's market leadership is based upon the simple and sound formula of gigantic volume, meager unit profit, rock-solid practical engineering and styling."

In December 1953, Chevrolet introduced revised versions of its Advance-Design trucks. The major changes were a new grille, one-piece windshield, larger-capacity engine, and the option of automatic transmission. Then, on October 28, 1954, the same versions were

*Above* **With the top down, this Bel Air illustrates the low-slung look sought by Harley Earl. The rear fender trim, enclosing the Bel Air name and Chevrolet crest, was only fitted to the Bel Air range. The stone guard behind the front wheel and the trim around the fuel filler flap are not standard, but all Bel Airs had fender skirts.**

*Below* **The dash has lots of chrome and a radio, while an electric clock was part of the Bel Air package.**

announced as carry-overs for the first quarter of 1955. Apart from a slight increase in price, the only alteration at this time was a change to a conventional open drive-shaft in place of the torque tube used previously. The end of the Advance-Design truck era came on March 25, 1955 with the release of a completely new series of Chevy trucks, the first since 1947.

The cross-bar grille is usually seen with a painted finish. Although a chrome plated version was offered by the factory, this was rather expensive, and few trucks seem to have been ordered with it. The other obvious

*Left* **All '54 Chevys have red and white taillight lenses, but back-up lights were optional and not connected unless ordered. The continental spare wheel mount is fashionable today, but was rare when the car was new.**
*Below* **Looking down on the truck gives a good impression of the shapely body: there's hardly a straight**

new feature was the curved, one-piece windshield. Of similar size to the earlier two-piece windshield, it came in clear or tinted glass and was said to increase comfort, safety and convenience, and to provide extra visibility.

Under the hood, the standard powerplant for the 3100 series was a 235.5cu.in Thriftmaster six with a higher compression ratio than before, producing 112hp at 3,700rpm. The optional automatic was not the Power-glide used in Chevy cars, but GM's tough Hydra-Matic four-speed.

In retrospect, the Chevy automobiles and trucks of

**line anywhere. Headlight "eyebrows" and the kerb feeler**

**on the running board are custom accessories.**

*Below* **The driver's side of the half-ton pick-up cab is**

**unadorned, apart from the "3100" badge. The three-**

**quarter-ton version has a "3600" nameplate and longer**

**wheelbase, but otherwise looks identical.**

**1954 CHEVROLET BEL AIR
TWO-DOOR CONVERTIBLE**

**Engine:**
OHV, inline six cylinder, cast-iron block and head
Capacity: 235.5cu.in (3.86 liters)
Bore and stroke: 3.56x3.94in
Compression ratio: 7.5:1
Power output: 115hp at 3,700rpm
Torque: 200lb/ft at 2,000rpm
Carburetor: Single Rochester one-barrel

**Transmission:**
Three-speed manual, column shift

**Chassis/body:**
Wheelbase: 115in
Overall length: 196.5in
Overall width: 75in
Shipping weight: 3,445lb
Suspension: Coil-spring independent front; leaf springs with torque-tube rear axle
Wheel diameter: 15in

**Performance:**
Top speed: 96mph
0-60mph: 18.1sec
Standing quarter mile: 20.7sec

**General:**
Factory price, 1954: $2,185
Production total: 8,156

*Above* **A foot operated starter switch is on the right of the clutch pedal, while the floor mounted gearshift lever came with the four-speed transmission.**

*Above* **The hood emblem was new for '54, while the Chevrolet name was spelled out in bold letters across the top of the grille.**

*Above* **From this angle, the '54 Chevy pick-up is almost indistinguishable from earlier models. The rear bumper was an option, but dual exhausts weren't on the list!**

1954 can be seen as representing the end of an age. For Chevrolet, it was an age dominated by the Stovebolt six-cylinder engine, an extremely rugged and reliable unit that had been in use since 1929, and which gained its place in American automotive folklore as "The Cast Iron Wonder". But the 1950s were becoming brighter and livelier, and cars needed performance to match the stratospheric designs created by their stylists. It was a time to look forward, not back. Sure, the old straight-six would continue for many years yet, but only as a lower-priced option in place of the new V8 engines to come.

It's unlikely that Joe Public recognized the transformation taking place at Chevrolet: the manufacturer of dependable, but mundane, family sedans was becoming the producer of some the hottest coupes and convertibles ever seen. There were pointers, of course - like the introduction of the Corvette - but to a large extent, these went unnoticed, or their significance was not fully appreciated by those outside the auto industry.

---

**1954 CHEVROLET SERIES 3100
HALF-TON PICK-UP TRUCK**

**Engine:**
OHV, inline six cylinder, cast-iron block and head
Capacity: 235.5cu.in (3.86 liters)
Bore and stroke: 3.56x3.94in
Compression ratio: 6.7:1
Power output: 112hp at 3,700rpm
Carburetor: Single Rochester one-barrel

**Transmission:**
Four-speed manual, floor shift

**Chassis/body:**
Wheelbase: 116in
Weight: 3,145lb
Suspension: Leaf springs front and rear; I-beam front axle and torque-tube rear axle
Wheel diameter: 16in

**General:**
Factory price, 1954: $1,419
Production total: 235,423*

*Production figure is total for all Chevrolet light-duty trucks and vans; no breakdown of Series 3100 pick-ups is available.

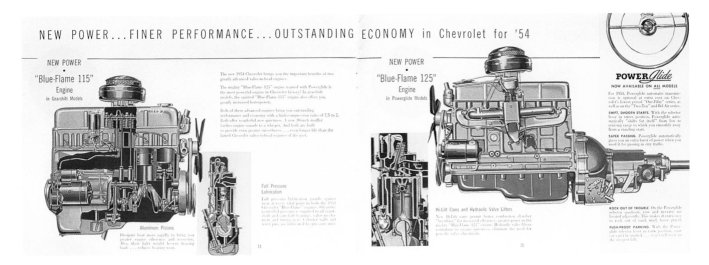

Above This Chevrolet sales brochure for 1954 explains the improvements made to engines, including full pressure lubrication, aluminum pistons, a high-lift cam and hydraulic lifters, and describes differences between the engines supplied in manual-transmission cars and those equipped with the Powerglide automatic. The mighty 125hp, Blue Flame straight-six is described as "the most powerful engine in Chevrolet history!", promising "outstanding performance and economy." Virtues of the automatic transmission, listed on the right, include "push-proof parking".

Below Smiles all round as the 31 millionth Chevrolet, a '54 Bel Air convertible, rolls off the Tarrytown, New York assembly line on June 23, 1954.

# 1955

## STEALING THE THUNDER OF THE HIGH PRICED CARS

Few auto manufacturers, if any, can have experienced a year like Chevrolet did in 1955. It was a milestone for the company, seeing the introduction of their fantastic new V8 engine, and was the first of three truly classic model years, which resulted in record shattering sales.

The foundations for the '55 Chevy were being laid as early as 1951, but the real architect of the brand-new car was Ed Cole, who arrived at Chevrolet in May 1952, taking the position of chief engineer. It was Cole's energy and enthusiasm that lit the creative fires at Chevrolet, and it can be argued that he, more than any other individual, was responsible for the transformation of the company's image so that it appealed to a younger and more performance oriented car buyer.

Cole's reputation within GM had been established at Cadillac, where he was involved in the development of the new overhead-valve V8 that was introduced in the 1949 models. Working closely with Chevy motor engineer Harry F. Barr, and using the same design principles employed at Cadillac, Cole came up with a powerplant

**Although a familiar and accepted design today, when introduced on October 28, 1954, the all-new 1955 Chevrolet was regarded as a somewhat radical departure from previous Chevy designs. Once accepted, however, cars like this Bel Air went on to sell in record numbers.**

that set standards which remained unequalled for many years. Lighter than the old Stovebolt six, the new 265cu.in engine produced more horsepower and revved to much higher rpm. It was to generate a whole new family of great Chevy V8 "small-blocks" that would keep the company ahead in the decades to come.

But it wasn't just the engine that was new; over in the body and chassis design departments, exciting things were also happening. Unlike most automobiles, which evolve gradually over a number of years, the '55 Chevrolets were virtually all brand-new, almost from the ground up. In fact, the only major components retained from the previous model year were the Powerglide automatic transmission, the straight-six engine and the manual gearbox. Everything else - chassis, suspension, rear

axle, body, and so on - was completely fresh and "state of the art" for 1955.

It was Clare "Mac" MacKichan, working under the head of General Motors Styling, Harley Earl, who was given the task of styling the body and interior of the '55 models, and there's no doubt that between them they produced a minor automotive masterpiece. The use of an expensive one-piece, wraparound windshield on low-priced Chevrolets was questioned by the accountants, but at the time, Earl was at the height of his power and insisted that it remained. Wise though that decision proved, he wasn't infallible, and his choice of grille design (supposedly copied from Ferrari), with its rectangular grid, didn't go down well in some quarters and was replaced with something more conventional in '56.

*Above* **Chevrolet's new "Turbo-Fire" V8 engine was universally praised, and its ease of maintenance commented on. Most components that need regular attention are readily accessible - except the spark plugs, which are hidden under the exhaust manifolds.**

*Left* **This view shows the horizontal trim strip that runs across the door from the front fender, and the white painted insert on the rear fender that was only found on Bel Airs. The Chevy crest and Bel Air name can be seen behind the upright trim, below the belt-line dip that became a regular styling feature on Chevys of the 1950s.**

*Below* **The front grille was copied from a Ferrari, at the instigation of Harley Earl, but was unpopular with some people and blamed for poor initial sales. A new design was readied for a mid-year change, but was held over for the '56 model when sales took off in December 1954.**

While the Chevrolet models were all new for '55, the company still kept the three distinct series used previously, although the names were altered. At the bottom of the pile, the One-Fifty utility range consisted of only four models (three sedans and a station wagon), which sold in relatively modest numbers. Next, came the middle priced Two-Ten series with six variations, including a couple of coupes. At the top were the Bel Air models. These featured more chrome and plusher upholstery, and comprised two sedans, a sport coupe, a four-door station wagon, a convertible and a two-door hardtop station wagon called the Nomad. Considered beautiful today, the Nomad cost $200 more than any other Chevrolet and never really caught on. The concept was dropped after '57, although the name continued in use.

*Above* **The hood ornament leaves no doubt as to the source of its designer's inspiration: aviation and space rocket themes were used on all GM cars in the 1950s.**
*Below* **Small "V" emblems beneath the rear lights show that this car is powered by the V8. Dual exhausts were part of the 180hp "Power Pack" option.**

Following its introduction on October 28, 1954, the new Chevy sold slowly to begin with, causing questions to be asked in the GM hierarchy. After a couple of months, however, the public had accepted the radical changes, and sales figures began to climb dramatically, reaching record levels by December. Eventually, they culminated in an astounding model year total of 1.7 million units - by far the best year of the decade for Chevy.

The automotive press were seemingly entranced by the '55, although reservations were expressed about the new V8 because it seemed almost too good to be true! Noted automotive journalist Roger Huntington, analyzing the Chevy engine in *Motor Life* remarked: "...everything on the new design is so simple and straightforward that you can't help but wonder if the thing will stay month after month, winter and summer, with the more elabo-

rate V8s...there's almost got to be a catch somewhere!" As we now know, Huntington's fears were groundless. Elsewhere, praise was heaped upon praise, with Walt Woron, of *Motor Trend*, commenting: "...there are so many good features about the car. It has exceptional handling qualities for an American production car. Its acceleration is better than all but the top performance cars...Its ride is improved..." Wrapping up his report, Woron stated: "The greatest compliment we could pay to this car (he tested a Two-Ten four-door sedan with a V8 and Powerglide) is that our praise is so high and our criticisms so minor that we find it hard to believe it's a descendant of previous Chevrolets."

Over at the Corvette factory in St Louis, meanwhile, things weren't looking nearly so rosy. Despite the new V8, Chevy's fiberglass two-seater still refused to sell in

*Above* **The glovebox was placed in the center of the dash to make it more accessible to both driver and passenger. However, the clock on the far right, under the Bel Air "fan", is well away from the driver's line of sight. As this particular Chevy was originally sold in Florida, it was ordered without a heater. The three auxiliary instruments, mounted on a panel under the dash, are not standard equipment.**

*Below* **The wide front bench seat and column mounted shifter give plenty of room for three people to ride in comfort. Even the corner of the double-curvature windshield doesn't intrude that much: there is no danger of banging your knee when exiting or entering the car, as on some models. The pedals are suspended from beneath the dash, instead of being floor mounted, as on previous cars.**

---

**1955 CHEVROLET BEL AIR
TWO-DOOR SEDAN**

**Engine:**
OHV V8, cast-iron block and heads
Capacity: 265cu.in (4.34 liters)
Bore and stroke: 3.75x3.00in
Compression ratio: 8.0:1
Power output: 162hp at 4,400rpm (Optional "Power Pack" engine with single four-barrel carburetor and dual exhausts was rated at 180hp at 4,600rpm)
Torque: 257lb/ft at 2,200rpm
Carburetor: Single Rochester two-barrel

**Transmission:**
Powerglide two-speed automatic

**Chassis/body:**
Wheelbase: 115in
Overall length: 195.6in
Overall width: 74in
Shipping weight: 3,140lb
Suspension: Coil-spring independent front; semi-elliptic leaf springs with live rear axle
Wheel diameter: 15in

**Performance:**
Top speed: 98mph
0-60mph: 12.3sec
Standing quarter mile: 19.0sec at 71mph

**General:**
Factory price, 1955: $1,987
Production total: 168,313

any sort of numbers, and only 700 were made. However, this was to be the last year for the original 1953 body design, and things were set to improve significantly thereafter, as GM elected to give the sports car one last chance. Advertising in various periodicals naturally emphasized the 'Vette's performance and handling, using phrases like "Loaded for bear" and "You can still buy magic!" But possibly the most fanciful piece of copywriting occurred when the V8 powered Corvette was compared to a V2 rocket: "...a stunning surge of acceleration, a seemingly limitless jet-stream of silken power. For most driving you can forget the bottom half of the accelerator: that's labelled 'for emergency use only.' But when you need it, mister, you've got it!" You'd have

*Below* **On November 23, 1954, a gold 1955 Chevrolet Bel Air two-door hardtop was paraded through the streets of Flint, Michigan to celebrate production of the 50 millionth General Motors car. As can be seen, huge crowds turned out to witness the event.**

thought that those few lines alone would have sold more than 700 cars.

On the truck side, 1955 saw Chevrolet introduce a whole new range of light-duty commercial vehicles under the "Task Force" banner. Arriving in dealerships for the launch on March 25, 1955, these second-series '55 trucks and vans looked totally different to the old Advance-Design models they replaced. Squarer in shape, with a wraparound windshield and egg-crate grille that matched the appearance of Chevy cars, Task Force trucks were just as radical a departure from the preceding year's designs as the automobiles.

The 3100 series half-ton trucks now had a 2in shorter wheelbase at 114in. One innovation in this group was the "suburbanite" pick-up, more popularly known as the Cameo. A limited-edition truck with slab-sided, fiberglass outer panels on the cargo bed, it represented Chevrolet's first attempt at marketing a dual-purpose vehicle that was suitable for both weekday load hauling and weekend leisure driving. In effect, the Cameo

*Above* "The Hot One" was the advertising slogan used to describe the new '55 Chevrolet. As if to confirm this assessment, a Bel Air convertible was chosen as the pace car for the 1955 Indianapolis 500.

*Below* This Chevrolet photograph uses an ingenious method to show the front and rear styling of the 1955 Cameo pick-up. The limited-edition truck was one of the first factory attempts at creating a practical dual-purpose vehicle. The grille design on the all-new Task Force trucks was similar to that used on Chevy cars.

opened up a whole new vista of automotive design, which is still growing over 40 years later.

The 1955 Chevrolet also became a focal point for a landmark in General Motors' history: the production of the 50 millionth GM vehicle. On November 23, 1954, a gold painted Bel Air two-door hardtop, with gold plated trim, rolled off the Flint, Michigan production line and was paraded through the city's streets in an 18-float cavalcade, dubbed the "GOLDEN CARnival", that received national television coverage. A further 5,000 Bel Air four-door sedans were painted Anniversary Gold to commemorate the occasion and shipped to dealers, but they did not sell very easily, and many were

*Above* **The Bel Air script and Chevy crest are below the characteristic dip at the base of the rear side window.**
*Below* **Although fitted with a later engine and custom wheels, this Coral and Shadow Gray '55 Nomad clearly shows why the model is so popular today. Despite its**

**attractive lines, however, the two-door hardtop wagon failed to sell in sufficient numbers and it was dropped for 1958. Since the roof was visible, Harley Earl decreed that indented "ribs" should be added to break up the expanse of sheet metal.**

resprayed to find buyers. Such was the economic influence of GM, that even president Dwight Eisenhower marked the occasion by saying that it epitomized "the industrial, scientific and creative genius of our people."

The importance of 1955 in Chevrolet history cannot be overstressed. It brought the company a bold new image that was to generate immediate success and ensure prosperity for the remainder of the decade, and well beyond. Banished forever was the idea that Chevrolet only built cars that grandma drove. A Bel Air convertible was used as the pace car for the 1955 Indy 500; from this year on, the bow-tie emblem became a symbol of the new vitality and spirit of the 1950s.

*Below* **The Nomad exhibits different styling to the other Chevy station wagons, the B-post being raked forward to give a more sporty look. None of the '55 Chevy station wagons has the beltline dip of the other cars, while the Nomad also has the Bel Air name and Chevrolet badge**

## Everything's NEW!

**GREAT NEW V8**

The valve-in-head eight as only the valve-in-head leader can build it! 162 horsepower with an 8-to-1 ultra-high compression ratio! Highly efficient oversquare design means less piston travel . . . less friction and wear. Exceptionally high horsepower per pound! The new Chevrolet V8 brings you brilliant performance, surprisingly high gas mileage, and extra-long life.

**TWO NEW SIXES**

The great new valve-in-head six teamed with Powerglide delivers full 136 h.p. And it features new efficiency and smoothness of operation, with new vibration-smothering 4-point suspension and new, more efficient cooling and lubrication systems. The spirited new 123-h.p. six, offered in gearshift models, brings you these same new advances.

positioned on the rear fin. Only 6,103 Nomads were produced, making it the rarest of all 1955 Chevrolets.

*Above* **"Everything's New!" shouted the Chevrolet sales brochure, describing the V8 engine in glowing terms and even calling the old six-cylinder engine "spirited".**

# 1956

## YOUTH, BEAUTY, CHEVROLET, ACTION!

After such a phenomenal year as 1955, it was to be expected that the pace would slow a little in '56 and, across the industry as a whole, sales dropped slightly. But Chevrolet came up with a winner again, and held on to the coveted number-one spot.

The 1956 Chevy models were hardly more than facelifted versions of the '55 cars, and they are often overlooked because of this. Among the obvious changes was the revised, full-width grille, which had been designed originally by Clare MacKichan and his staff as a mid-year modification for the '55 model when GM management hit the panic button over poor early sales. When sales picked up, the idea of an interim design change was dropped, but the new grille became part of the revamp for the '56 model year. Extra side body trim and reshaped wheel openings, plus large rectangular parking lamps and small round lenses for the rear lights made up the other more apparent parts of the redesign. In fact, practically the whole bottom half of the car (apart from the doors) was updated at tremendous cost, estimated to be as much as $40 million!

**The design brief for the '56 Chevy, given to stylist Clare MacKichan, specified a more imposing front end. The grille was originally intended as a mid-year alteration to the '55 models, but was held over when sales picked up.**

In later years, in an interview with *Collectible Automobile* magazine, MacKichan said that the styling brief for '56 specified a "more imposing front end and a little more chrome on the sides", both of which were undeniably achieved. He was also quoted as saying that Harley Earl wasn't above changing his mind about styling features, and many times he heard him remark that you need "entertainment" on the side of a car. There's plenty of that on the '56 Chevy!

The influence of styling on new car sales cannot be underestimated, but neither can that of performance on the open road. In this latter respect, the '56 Chevrolet proved second to none. To press home the point, adverts declared: "The Hot One's Even Hotter", and "Loves to Go...And Looks It!" The horsepower race was on in earnest, and Chevy started the year in pole position, having pepped up the 265cu.in V8 to 205hp in Super Turbo-Fire form, thanks to the Power Pack consisting of a four-barrel carburetor, high-lift camshaft, dual exhausts and 9.25:1 compression. Even when Ford increased the performance of their engines to match, Chevy was able to play a trump card by offering the top Corvette engine as an option in all their passenger cars. With dual four-barrel carbs, solid instead of hydraulic lifters, a "Duntov" cam and cylinder heads with larger ports, the numbers now read 225hp at 5,200rpm.

Ah yes, the Corvette! Thanks to legendary engineer Zora Arkus-Duntov, and the styling influence of the aforementioned Harley Earl, the Corvette at last looked and performed like a real sports car should. Recognizing the shortcomings in the original design, Earl ensured that proper wind-up windows replaced the crude side curtains, and exterior door handles were fitted at the outset. To improve the overall shape and give the '56 Corvette a more purposeful look, the new body was made cleaner and without the styling gimmicks of the earlier version. Distinctive concave panels, extend-

*Above* **Although the basic body shell - new in 1955 - remained the same in '56, detail changes were made, and several new body types were introduced. This Bel Air two-door hardtop, or sport coupe, is typical of the more popular body styles.**

*Left* **Although the continental spare dominates the rear of this '56 Bel Air, the most significant change can be found in the lights, which have bullet-shaped lenses.**

*Right* **The 265cu.in Chevy Super Turbo-Fire V8 put out 205hp, thanks to a high-lift cam, 9.25:1 compression ratio, a four-barrel carburetor and other refinements.**

*Above* **The dash retains the dual-cowl look, although the mesh design matches the front grille, replacing the hundreds of miniature bow-tie emblems used in '55.**
*Below* **Alterations to the '56 Chevy body design looked subtle, but were enough to make the car seem like a new model. Nassau Blue/Harbor Blue was one of 13 two-tone color combinations available for '56 sport coupes; there were ten single colors to choose from as well!**

ing back across the doors from the front wheel openings, were introduced and remained a feature until 1962. The grille kept its teeth, which became a 'Vette trademark that also lasted into the 1960s. A pair of small fake air inlet scoops, positioned on top of the front fenders, in front of the windshield, may be seen as a retrograde step, but these were removed after '57.

However, it was Duntov's wizardry that really turned things around. No mean driver himself, he recorded a two-way average speed of 150.58mph in a specially modified '56 Corvette on the sand at Daytona Beach in Florida. Thanks to his expertise, the road car was no slouch either, 100mph being possible in second gear, with a top speed approaching 130mph. The three-speed manual transmission was a vast improvement on the Powerglide automatic, although this was still available for those who had less sporting pretensions. While the

drum brakes remained inadequate for high-speed work, and the handling wasn't quite up to European sports car standards (although it was good for an American car), at least the Corvette could now compete successfully on the race track and build the performance image required to boost sales. And a total of 3,467 were made, ensuring that Chevrolet would keep the Corvette in production for the duration.

The Corvette wasn't the only Chevrolet that saw competitive action in '56: the passenger cars also set speed records and won races. Smokey Yunick took a quartet of '56 Chevys to the 1.3-mile oval at Darlington, South Carolina, and one set a 24hr record average speed for a US production car of 101.58mph, beating Chrysler's previous record by almost 12mph. Vince Piggins, a name that would become synonymous with Chevy performance in the muscle car era of the 1960s, had arrived

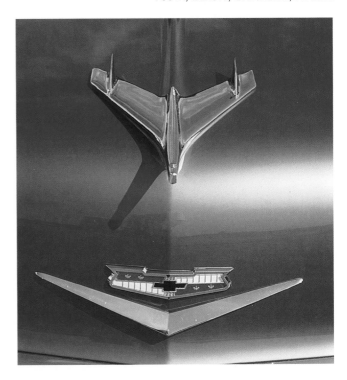

*Above* **The aeronautical theme continued in the design of the hood emblem for '56, although its wings were trimmed slightly.**

**1956 CHEVROLET BEL AIR
TWO-DOOR SPORT COUPE**

**Engine:**
OHV V8, cast-iron block and heads
Capacity: 265cu.in (4.34 liters)
Bore and stroke: 3.75x3.00in
Compression ratio: 9.25:1
Power output: 205hp at 4,600rpm
Torque: 268lb/ft at 3,000rpm
Carburetor: Single four-barrel

**Transmission:**
Powerglide two-speed automatic

**Chassis/body:**
Wheelbase: 115in
Overall length: 197.5in
Overall width: 73.7in
Shipping weight: 3,212lb
Suspension: Coil-spring independent front; semi-elliptic leaf springs with live rear axle
Wheel diameter: 15in

**Performance:**
Top speed: 108mph
0-60mph: 10.7sec
Standing quarter mile: 18.3sec at 76mph

**General:**
Factory price, 1956: $2,275
Production total: 128,382

at Chevrolet Engineering from Hudson and took charge of the preparation of three cars entered in the annual Pike's Peak hillclimb. Jerry Unser Jr piloted a Chevy to first place in the stock car category of this event, climbing the 12 miles of twisting dirt road to the finish line at an altitude of 14,110ft in 16min, 8sec - over a minute quicker than the time set by Zora Arkus-Duntov at the wheel of another Chevy in 1955. Chevrolets also finished second, fifth, sixth and tenth in the "race to the clouds" - an impressive showing.

Although speed and styling were the name of the game in '56, Chevrolet also added several safety features: "crashproof" door locks were standard across the range; a padded dash was introduced; and seat belts were offered as optional extras. However, these items received little publicity, for road test reports concentrat-

*Below* **This Bel Air convertible, in Adobe Beige and Sierra Gold, has standard wheel covers and unadorned bumpers. After station wagons, convertibles were the most expensive of the '56 Chevy models, at $2,443.**

ed on the car's performance. *Road & Track* magazine concluded: "In short, the 1956 Chevrolet is an even better performer than last year and equally important, it handles slightly better."

Handling seems to have been a preoccupation of some test drivers. One of the more adventurous *Road & Track* staff, who obviously believed in pushing things to the limit, wrote of the '56 Chevy: "...it can be cornered at speeds which closely approach that of a vigorously driven sports car, but the operation demands dexterity, muscles and 'grit' bordering on the foolhardy." Precisely which sports car he was referring too wasn't made clear, but it sounds like a real "white knuckle" experience! More concise was Jim Lodge, of *Motor Trend*, who summed up his impressions thus: "In power and performance, in appearance and trade-in value, Chevy is keeping the competition on its toes."

The extensive options list was an important part of Chevrolet's marketing policy, and if few people would choose air conditioning at a whopping $430 (nearly 20 percent of the list price of an average '56 Chevy), then

*Above* **Two workers buff the paintwork on a Two-Ten sedan. Note the words "No heater" written on the windshield, which presumably meant that this car was destined for a hot state like California or Florida.**

*Below* **Chevrolet offered sedan deliveries throughout the 1950s, but they only sold in small numbers. This 1956 One-Fifty sedan delivery is based on the two-door Handyman station wagon and has a rear liftgate.**

*Above* **The Corvette renaissance happened in 1956 with this very attractive re-design, rated by many enthusiasts as the definitive 'Vette among the early models. While its ancestry was obvious, the clever alterations produced a new and exciting image. When painted in a contrasting** color, as here, the scooped "coves" in the body sides become prominent features, but elsewhere much was changed from the original. With the base price held at the '55 level, plus the V8 engine, it's no wonder that sales rocketed to 3,467 units.

*Below* **Corvette performance was boosted by a 225hp version of the 265cu.in V8. Dual four-barrel Carter carbs, 9.25:1 compression ratio, solid-lifter Duntov camshaft and larger ports provided the extra power.**

power brakes at $38 and power steering for $92 looked much more attractive. Even Cadillac's Autronic Eye automatic headlight dipper was in the Chevy catalog for $44.25, but prices started as low as $1.60 for a vanity mirror fixed to the internal sun visor. In all, nearly 60 items were available, from floor mats to an electric shaver, and they produced millions of dollars in extra revenue for the company.

On the truck front, only detail changes were made for '56, the second model year of the Task Force design beginning on February 1. The badge on the front of the hood was wider and set lower down, closer to the top of the grille, and incorporated a large "V" under the bow-tie emblem if the truck had a V8 engine. The nameplates

*Above* **The optional removable hardtop is not only functional, but its clean lines also add to the overall attractive appearance of the Corvette. Although two people are needed to remove or install the top, once in place, it provides good all-round vision, with plenty of** space behind the driver and passenger. Proper wind-up windows make for a fully weatherproof and practical car. The rear lights were changed for '56 and kept within the body contours, while the rear license plate was mounted below the bumper.

on the front fenders were also relocated above the crease line. Apart from that and some extra colors, the major news concerned increased power for both six- and eight-cylinder engines, even a 205hp Super Turbo-Fire engine being made available later in the year - performance trucks had arrived! Surprisingly, after a good showing in '55, when well over 5,000 Cameo pick-ups were sold, demand fell alarmingly to less than a third of that total for '56. Looking back, it's difficult to figure out why, since the truck was still attractive and, with the hotter engines, produced a potent package.

In the numbers game, Chevrolet was still ahead of the field in both passenger cars and trucks...but for some, the best was yet to come.

*Below* **Apart from the steering wheel, very little of the Corvette's interior was changed for '56. The dashboard layout is virtually identical to the previous models, retaining the dual-cowl design used in full-sized Chevys.**

# 1957

## THE MOST POPULAR USED CAR IN HISTORY

What can be written about the 1957 Chevrolet that hasn't been said already many times before? In automotive terms, it is almost unique. Ever since its introduction on October 17, 1956, the '57 Chevy has enjoyed phenomenal popularity, and now, over 40 years later, there are enough specialist restorers and suppliers of reproduction parts that it would almost be possible to build a complete new car from scratch. No other 1950s car - and arguably few from any other decade - enjoys such a fervent and widespread following.

Why is this? At first glance, it's difficult to understand: the '57 Chevy was basically a three-year-old body shell with a substantial facelift and a V8 engine that was smaller than both the Ford and Plymouth competition. However, those bare facts pale into insignificance when you are confronted with the car itself. Quite simply, it is a masterpiece on wheels that became a 1950s icon.

Of course, creating an everlasting symbol of the age was far from the minds of the design staff engaged in

**This pristine Matador Red '57 Chevy Bel Air convertible displays the striking looks that are as popular today as when the car was launched. Rear fender skirts were optional extras, which seem more in vogue in the nostalgia-ridden 1990s than they probably ever were in the 1950s, but who cares? They look great anyway!**

the day-to-day toil of producing the thousands of drawings needed. Indeed, Chevrolet's styling studio head, Clare MacKichan, reckoned that the final '57 design included several ideas that had been rejected on the '56 version! Continuity of development doesn't seem to have been much of a priority back then, and sometimes even totally outrageous suggestions could be incorporated if it was felt that they looked right.

However, it seemed that some features had been on the drawing board for quite a while. Illustrations completed in the studio in 1949 showed a front end treatment uncannily like the '57 bumper, while designer Carl Renner apparently produced a drawing in 1953 that also matched the finished '57 design. Although the massive bumper was undoubtedly a distinctive component, the most noticeable change from preceding models was the car's longer, lower look - a direct result of Harley Earl's insistence that it made cars more attractive. One of the consequences of producing a lower profile was the adoption of an unusual ventilation system, which had fresh air inlets positioned above the headlights, rather than in the cowl below the windshield, thereby allowing a reduced hood height.

The hood, bereft of the normal airplane inspired ornament, came with twin harpoon-like decorations, which were intended to increase the illusion of a smoother and lower appearance. Overall, the '57 body revamp was so cleverly handled that not only did it look totally new against the '56, but it was also regarded as a whole lot better. The rear fenders had sharp, but fairly modest,

*Right* **Even with the top raised, the '57 Bel Air has a sporty look that came from the designers' continual efforts to make cars look lower and longer than previous models. This policy was directed by Harley Earl, who believed that it produced more appealing automobiles, and few would argue with the results.**

*Left* **Twin projectile-shaped windsplitz set in the hood were a complete departure from the airplane inspired hood ornaments that had been used previously, and were among the methods used to keep the hood profile as low as possible.**

*Right* **Probably the most unusual features of the '57 Chevy front end are the air inlets above the headlights, which are part of an extraordinary ventilation system designed to reduce the hood and cowl height. Black rubber "buffers" were optional extras that are proving favorite items today, as they can prevent accidental damage at slow speeds, plus they look pretty spiffy!**

*Left* **The '57 Chevy has a dominating countenance that some observers attributed to Cadillac influence; more critical commentators thought it looked rather heavy compared to the '56. Bumper guards were optional.**

*Right* **The Bel Air script and Chevy crest remained on the rear fin for 1957, but were mounted in the silver anodized aluminum trim panel. The use of gold on badges was another feature restricted to Bel Airs.**

*Below* **Although there was a choice of 16 colors for the body, and five for the top, no two-tone paint schemes were offered for the convertible.**

chrome-tipped fins which, on Bel Air models, featured one of the most effective styling devices developed during the 1950s: wedge-shaped, ribbed, anodized aluminum panels.

Interiors and dashboard layout were new, of course, and the extensive options list contained as many gizmos as before, but the really big news after the redesigned bodies concerned engines - and fuel injection. Manufactured by Rochester Carburetor Inc, after they had carried out a test and modification program on an original GM design, the Ramjet mechanical fuel injection unit seemed quite a breakthrough, being said to produce more horsepower and better fuel economy. However, the Ramjet was far from trouble free under normal driving conditions: dirt blocked the fuel nozzles and heat absorption caused rough idling. At the end of the '58 model year, it was withdrawn as a mainstream Chevy passenger-car option, although the Corvette list continued to include fuel injection (a revised and improved version) until 1965.

Under the Ramjet (which, incidentally, cost $550 - a considerable chunk of money in '57) was an enlarged V8, displacing 283cu.in (4.64 liters) thanks to a 0.125in larger bore. With this engine and the fuel injection, Chevy were able to brag about generating 1hp/cu.in - considered a performance milestone at the time, although Chrysler had already achieved the same output level with their Hemi V8. No matter who actually recorded that particular figure first, the Chevy was still a fast car for its day, and one that easily outpaced the opposition - exceeding l00mph and hitting 60mph in 11sec when only equipped with the base V8 and Powerglide automatic.

If the Ramjet fuel injection can be regarded as a rather limited success, the new Turboglide automatic was little short of a disaster. Modeled on Buick's Dynaflow transmission, the Turboglide was smoother shifting and

weighed less than the Powerglide, but it was more costly to build. Unfortunately, the Turboglide was also prone to failure and difficult to fix. Chevy kept it as an option until the end of the '61 model year, before dropping it and offering the trusty Powerglide as the only automatic transmission. Quite why they embarked on the Turboglide project in the first place isn't really clear, as other divisions within GM were already using the excellent Hydra-Matic, which eventually was adopted by Chevrolet as well.

These few quibbles aside, nothing can detract from the feeling that, in 1957, Chevrolet produced a package that was absolutely right. Therefore, the fact that Chevy failed to dominate the market in the same manner as before seems rather curious. Indeed, model year figures show that Ford actually outsold Chevy by quite a few thousand, while on the calendar year numbers, they

*Above left* **Chevy rear tailfins are quite restrained when compared to other Detroit offerings from 1957. The rear light and back-up light are neatly integrated in a chrome housing that forms part of the bumper. The ribbed and anodized aluminum infill panel is only found on Bel Airs.**
*Above right* **Chevy switched from 15in to 14in wheels in '57 and fitted low-pressure tires. These changes reduced the height of the cars by about 0.5in - a small, but important, contribution to an overall lower profile.**
*Left* **Chevrolet script on the trunk was in gold for the Bel Air. The "V" emblem signifies a V8 engine.**
*Right* **For 1957, the dashboard layout was changed completely, with no attempt to produce a balanced design. The instruments are higher to make them easier to read, while the glovebox is still fairly central and the clock remains on the far right. The red and silver patterned vinyl upholstery is one of four color combinations exclusive to Bel Air convertibles, but fuzzy dice definitely were not part of the package!**

were almost neck and neck, Chevrolet being ahead by the narrowest of margins. In truth, the battle for customers was becoming tougher than ever and, despite price reductions, 1957 was not the bumper year predicted by the auto industry. In fact, toward the tail end of '57, the beginnings of the economic slump, which was to drastically reduce US car sales in 1958, began to take effect, with a consequent sharp drop in demand.

Except for Corvette orders, that is. While the styling was virtually unchanged, the new "Fuelie" engine and Borg-Warner four-speed manual transmission made the '57 'Vette a very hot prospect indeed. Sales almost doubled, with over 6,000 sports cars leaving the St Louis assembly plant. Given a 0-60mph time of under 6sec, and a top speed of over 130mph, the success of the '57 Corvette was hardly surprising. Nor can its competition outings have done any harm: in the GT class at Sebring,

## 1957 CHEVROLET BEL AIR
## TWO-DOOR CONVERTIBLE

**Engine:**
OHV V8, cast-iron block and heads
Capacity: 283cu.in (4.64 liters)
Bore and stroke: 3.875x3.00in
Compression ratio: 9.5:1
Power output: 220hp at 4,800rpm
Carburetor: Single four-barrel

**Transmission:**
Powerglide two-speed automatic

**Chassis/body:**
Wheelbase: 115in
Overall length: 200in
Shipping weight: 3,405lb
Suspension: Coil-spring independent front; leaf springs with live rear axle
Wheel diameter: 14in

**Performance:**
Top speed: 111mph
0-60mph: 9.9sec
Standing quarter mile: 17.5sec at 77.5mph

**General:**
Factory price, 1957: $2,611
Production total: 47,562

for example, 'Vettes came first and second, 20 laps ahead of the nearest Mercedes.

With all this factory backed racing activity, a major setback occurred when the Automobile Manufacturers' Association issued an edict in June 1957, effectively banning their members from participating in competition. However, while the guys in the Chevy front office were toeing the official AMA line and proclaiming that they were no longer in racing, out back, there was plenty of unofficial help for those drivers who could put a Chevrolet into the winner's circle.

*Below* **Station wagons grew in popularity during the 1950s, and Chevrolet produced plenty of them. This Beauville four-door wagon was from the Two-Ten range. Over 214,000 Chevy station wagons were built in 1957, 21,083 of them being nine-passenger Beauvilles.**

Having a recognized race car driver test a new car isn't a new idea, and *Speed Age* asked stock car ace Johnnie Tolan to try out the '57 Chevy. Tolan drove a Bel Air four-door sedan through the Los Angeles rush-hour congestion, and also took it to the track before announcing: "...I was impressed with the new Chevy, liked its looks as well as its performance..." Likewise, in *Motor Trend*, Pete Molson reported that the Chevrolet was still the hottest car in its field, commenting that the extra performance "might be abused by the power-happy", but that it was "capable of keeping you and your family out

*Below* **How many men does it take to fit a front bumper to a 1957 Chevrolet? Well, there are five in this assembly-line photo, and you can bet that none of them had time to spare, because as soon as this car had gone, another would be waiting.**

*Above* **To obtain the 283cu.in capacity for the V8 engine, its bore diameter was enlarged by 0.125in. An optional four-barrel carburetor, 9.5:1 compression ratio and other modifications pushed output to 220hp. No wonder Chevy advertised the '57 as "Sweet, Smooth and Sassy!"**

*Above* **This customized '57 Series 3100 step-side pick-up gives an idea of the differences between the ordinary trucks and the Cameo. Twin windsplitz on the hood were new, and accessory "projectile" ornaments (similar to those on the passenger cars) were optional extras.**

*Below* **Obvious changes to the Cameo included a new grille and hood emblem, and relocation of the side badges. Standard colors were ivory and red, but there was also a choice of nine two-tone schemes, among them Cardinal Red over Arabian Ivory, seen here.**

of trouble." James Whipple, writing in the February 1957 issue of *Car Life*, suggested that drivers would need "quicker reactions and better judgement than ever before" to handle the extra power. *Motor Life* reported that the Chevy "belted out acceleration times that power-kitted versions of rival makes would find it hard to meet", and carried the message: "Chevrolet's strong points for 1957 are quality and performance."

While horsepower and performance captured the attention of the media, it must not be forgotten that Chevrolet still offered the 235cu.in inline-six as a base engine (producing 140hp), and a 162hp, 265cu.in V8 for those who weren't in that much of a hurry. The three model series - One-Fifty, Two-Ten and Bel Air - were retained, and while today's collector car market might prefer the more exotic coupes and convertibles, in 1957, the four-door sedans sold better than anything else.

Truckwise, Chevy offered four-wheel drive, a new grille and a hood with twin windsplitz moulded into the

top. "Bombsight" chrome ornaments could be ordered to dress-up the front of the windsplitz and provide a link with the passenger-car models. The four-wheel-drive trucks employed a 235cu.in, straight-six Thriftmaster engine and a four-speed manual transmission, but elsewhere the V8 powerplant was offered in Trademaster 265 and Taskmaster 283cu.in configurations, the latter only in larger vehicles.

The headlines in 1957 newspapers were full of doom, following the epoch making launch of the Soviet Union's Sputnik I satellite. The USSR had been the first to enter the space age and had gained a demoralizing lead over US technology. Meanwhile, the arrival of rock 'n' roll music caused conflict between teenagers and the older generation, while confrontations of a more serious nature were taking place over racial integration. There was plenty of other news, both good and bad, but in purely automotive terms, the year will always be remembered for the birth of a Chevrolet classic.

*Above* **New on '57 Cameos was a contrasting color band on the side panel and chrome trim on the leading edge.**
*Below* **The "V" emblem on the door denotes that this truck is equipped with the optional V8; a similar "V" is incorporated in the badge on the front of the hood. Rated at a half-ton load capacity, the Cameo has a 78in bed and taillights similar to the '54 Chevy passenger cars, but with flat lenses. Back-up lights were standard. Only 2,572 Cameos were produced in 1957, less than half the amount built in '55.**

# 1958

## SERENITY...BY DESIGN!

After the outstanding success of 1957, it was almost inevitable that 1958 would be an anticlimax. The completely new Chevrolets introduced in October 1957 failed to sell as well as their immediate predecessors, and have not achieved anything like the same collectible status. However, while the blame for this demise can be attributed to the larger, heavier and slower designs of '58, one shouldn't ignore the circumstances in which they were produced.

With lead times for new automobile designs in the 1950s being measured in years, the specification for the 1958 models would have been prepared in the boom times of 1955 and 1956, when sales were at record levels and customers appeared to be demanding ever larger and more expensive cars. Unfortunately, the production planners couldn't have foreseen the downturn in the US economy, which began in the summer of 1957 and had become a full-blown recession by the fall, remaining in this depressed state throughout most of 1958. The

**Chevrolet styling changed completely for 1958, and the Impala was a new model - part of the top-of-the-range Bel Air series. Dual headlights appeared across the entire Chevy line-up. The lavish use of chrome on the front end is characteristic of the designs that emanated from General Motors' studios during this period.**

92

market for large, middle- to upper-priced cars evaporated in favor of smaller, cheaper models. In effect, the goal posts had been moved.

Despite this turn of events, Chevrolet would weather the storm far better than either Ford or Chrysler. Ford, of course, launched the Edsel in September 1957, with disastrous consequences, while at the same time, Chrysler were witnessing the dramatic decline of DeSoto, which ultimately would lead to its demise in November 1960. Overall, in 1958, car sales dropped by about 20 percent compared to the previous three years.

Not all makes and models suffered, however, and there were a few notable exceptions. Chevrolet's own Corvette, for instance, achieved a significant advance with over 9,000 units sold. Its direct rival, the Ford Thunderbird, had grown much larger for '58 and picked up sales, from 21,000 the previous year to nearly 38,000. But neither car could be said to be in the mass market, although the T-Bird was moving in that direction. The one name that really bucked the downward trend was lowly Rambler. Formed by the merger of Nash and Hudson in April 1954, American Motors Corporation re-introduced the Rambler badge (and, more importantly, the compact Rambler American model) just at the right time, more than doubling sales in 1958.

Clearly, the arrival of the larger, more rounded and more expensive Chevrolets was hardly well timed. Completely restyled and re-engineered, being based on a new "Safety Girder" chassis with a 2.5in-longer wheelbase and coil-spring suspension all round, the '58 cars were immediately distinguishable because of the dual-headlight front end. At the rear, the sharp fins had gone, being replaced by curved corners and taillights arranged horizontally, to match the front parking lights. With all the extra body trim (much of it aluminum), the Chevys had lost their clean, sporty look, and taken on a much more baroque appearance.

*Left* **The center of the Impala's steering wheel displays crossed flags and a caricature of the African antelope that gave its name to the car, while the glovebox bears the model name.**

*Right* **The radio speaker, in the center of the sculpted rear seat, also carries the Impala script, crossed flags and leaping antelope motif.**

*Below* **The wheelbase was increased by 2.5in, and '58 Chevys were larger all around. This particular car's front end sits nearer the ground than normal, thanks to a 3in lowering job; the wheels are non-standard, too. Apart from those changes, the car's appearance is correct.**

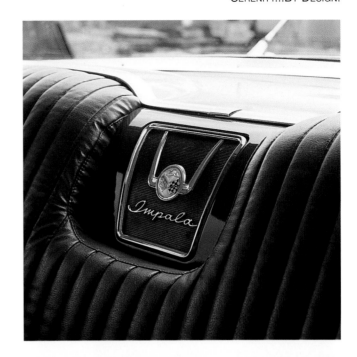

Also gone were the numerical designations for the middle and lower ranges. The cheapest Chevrolets were now called Del Ray, while the middle-priced models carried the Biscayne label; Bel Air still referred to the top-of-the-line cars. An important newcomer in '58 was the Impala. Available only as a two-door sport coupe or convertible, it featured all the Bel Air equipment, plus extra identifying insignia, dummy chrome air scoops in front of the rear wheel openings, and a race-style steering wheel. The Impala name would be around for quite a while, and it was re-introduced a couple of years ago as part of the 1994 Chevrolet line-up.

*Left* **Impala badging on the rear fender and a fake side air scoop, simulated by chrome trim, are exclusive to Impala models.**

*Below* **The rear view contrasts starkly with the previous year's design and went against the trend of taller and more exaggerated tailfins that was the industry norm.**

Although the 265/283cu.in V8 had already proved to be an excellent engine, by 1958, Chevy were losing out in the numbers game, as both Ford and Plymouth were offering powerplants with much larger capacities. Apparently not wanting to stretch the small-block any further for the moment (it would eventually grow through 327 and 350cu.in to 400cu.in), Chevrolet introduced the 348cu.in engine. Among the more unusual features of this engine were the 16-degree angled faces on top of the block, which formed wedge-shaped combustion chambers, the cylinder heads being virtually flat. This design caused problems later on when engines needed

**Extra embellishments on Impala models include six rear lights and a dummy vent in the roof. The Chevrolet script and "V" emblem on the trunk lid also differ from other models in the Bel Air range.**

*Below* **An Impala sport coupe comes to the end of the assembly line.**

## 1958 CHEVROLET IMPALA TWO-DOOR SPORT COUPE

**Engine:**
OHV V8, cast-iron block and heads
Capacity: 348cu.in (5.70 liters)
Bore and stroke: 4.125x3.25in
Compression ratio: 9.5:1
Power output: 250hp at 4,400rpm
Torque: 355lb/ft at 2,800rpm
Carburetor: Single four-barrel

**Transmission:**
Powerglide two-speed automatic

**Chassis/body:**
Wheelbase: 117.5in
Overall length: 209in
Overall width: 77.7in
Shipping weight: 3,684lb
Suspension: Coil springs all round; independent front, live axle rear
Wheel diameter: 14in

**Performance:**
Top speed: 100+mph
0-60mph: 10.1sec

**General:**
Factory price, 1958: $2,693
Production total: 142,592*

*Total of all 1958 Chevrolet two-door sport coupes; no breakdown of Impala model figures available.

*Left* **A spacious front bench seat and masses of legroom - the '58 Chevy is a car of generous proportions. The large glovebox is in the middle of the dash, while a clock is on the extreme right.**

*Right* **Dual rear light clusters are found on all '58 Chevy passenger cars, apart from Impalas and station wagons. Ordinary Bel Airs are devoid of the roof and fender trim found on Impalas, while other differences include the trunk badge and the position of the model name on the rear fender. Six-cylinder cars have single exhausts. Twin radio antennas are unlikely to be original equipment.**

reboring, and a special spacer plate had to be developed for use on the boring machines. The bigger engine worked well in its day, especially the 315hp version, which had a triple two-barrel carb set-up and 11.0:1 compression. *Motor Trend* achieved 0-60mph in 9.1sec and a quarter-mile time of 16.5sec with this engine. However, a '57 Chevy with a 283cu.in V8 and Ramjet fuel injection was quicker.

Most contemporary magazine road tests of 1958 Impalas concentrated on cars fitted with Chevy's Level-Air suspension system which, although it found favor with the journalists, failed to survive very long, as it was prone to trouble when subjected to the abuses of everyday motoring. Not that there was anything wrong with the standard coil-spring suspension; in fact, it drew plenty of praise. For example, Jim Whipple, of *Car Life*, declared: "My first drive in the Bel Air left me pretty much speechless...Seldom have I ever felt such a tremendous improvement in riding qualities as in the '58 Chevy..." Whipple summed up his road test report with these words: "The '58 Chevy is a good-looking, extremely comfortable and steady-riding car with powerful and quiet performance."

As mentioned earlier, Corvette sales showed a healthy increase in 1958, rising by almost 50 percent to 9,168 units. Less healthy was the Corvette's increase in size and weight. Adopting the same quad-headlight configuration as the full-size Chevy cars, the 'Vette body

*Left* **This four-door sedan represents the most popular Chevy body style for 1958: despite their new found performance image, the majority of Chevrolets were still bought as family transport. Total production of four-door models that year was 491,441. Although this is a top-of-the-line Bel Air, it could still be ordered with the old Stovebolt straight-six engine, as illustrated by the lack of a "V" emblem under the bow-tie shield on the hood.**

grew 3in wider and 10in longer, and gained 100lb. This was literally Harley Earl's last fling with the sports car he had brought into being (Earl retired from GM in 1959), and many people have criticized his final design for being over-elaborate and too heavy looking. Certainly, his successor, Bill Mitchell, took immediate steps to remove as much of the excess as he could, but it wasn't until the 1961 model that he was able to exert his influence to the full.

The '58 Corvette has a couple of features that are unique to that year: fake louvers in the hood and two bold chrome strips that run down the trunk lid to the rear bumper. Both of these non-functional items were removed for the following year. More durable of Earl's

*Above* **The taillight lenses of the '58 Corvette were designed to follow the body contours. Another styling feature unique to this 'Vette are the twin chrome ribs that run across the trunk lid. The exhaust openings in the rear bumper are oval in shape.**

*Right* **Without the small fake inlet scoops on the tops of the front fenders, the car's lines are a lot cleaner. However, the stylist's obsession with dummy air ducts wasn't quite over, and they were introduced to the front of the body side coves, behind the front wheel openings. In this instance, the design feature works quite well; it remained on Corvettes into the 1960s.**

*Above right* **In common with the other 1958 Chevrolets, the Corvette has quad headlights, while the hood is decorated with fake louvers (thankfully, they were removed for the '59 model). The front grille contains fewer vertical teeth, and the bumpers are more substantial, being fixed to the chassis to provide better protection when parking. Although the body is larger and heavier than the previous model, this did not have an adverse effect on sales, which rose to 9,168 units - the best annual total so far.**

final design ideas were the dual headlights and the reversed air scoops behind the front wheel openings, both of which remained in place until the last of this body shape in 1962. Other changes included a much overdue revamp of the interior, the dashboard layout being improved, and some slightly more powerful engines. In a test of four different-specification 1958 Corvettes for *Motor Trend*, retired racing driver Sam Hanks wrote: "Any way you look at it, I think the Chevrolet designers should be proud of the style of the Corvette, and their engineers should be proud of a fine sports car."

Four headlights also appeared on Chevy light-duty trucks in 1958, as did a new name - Apache. In fact, there was quite a new look to Chevrolet pick-ups, thanks

to a heavily restyled front end, although the cab and chassis structure was basically the same as before. Most of the components behind the cab remained unchanged, too, particularly on step-side models. The Cameo Carrier (as it was now called) was available for a few months of the 1958 model year, but after 1,405 of these expensive, limited-edition pick-ups had been made, it was discontinued. The reason for dropping the Cameo was that Chevy had a new, all-steel Fleetside ready to compete with Ford's Styleside pick-up, which

was already capturing a large chunk of the market. The Fleetside stood out by virtue of its cargo box sides, which had concave upper portions, a torpedo-shaped bulge just above the rear wheel opening, and a chrome Fleetside emblem positioned towards the back.

The Apache name was used on all Chevy light-duty trucks with gross vehicle weights of under 9,000lb, while Viking and Spartan denoted the medium- and heavy-duty ranges. Power for the trucks came from a 135hp Thriftmaster six or a 160hp Trademaster 283cu.in V8

*Above* **The Apache name was introduced in 1958 and used to describe all of Chevrolet's light-duty trucks. Series identification was shortened to two digits; this is a 3100 model.**

*Left* **All Chevy trucks had new front ends for 1958, with four headlights, although the basic chassis and cab structure remained as before. The grille featured a heavy horizontal center bar with large rectangular parking lights at each end, and there was a new design of emblem on the leading edge of the hood. This customized 3100 step-side has extra chrome and aluminum wheels, and it sits lower, but the overall shape remains stock.**

*Below* **A wedge-shaped instrument panel was installed on all Task Force trucks between 1955 and 1959. The chrome control knobs are part of the optional Custom Cab package.**

with a single two-barrel carburetor. The choice of transmissions was reduced when the overdrive option was withdrawn, but other new extras included Cool-Pack air conditioning and factory installed seat belts.

This was a bad year for the US auto industry as a whole, but Chevrolet still came out on top in both passenger-car and commercial-vehicle sales. The design of '58 Chevys had gone against the trend of ever larger tailfins, but it was only a temporary step out of line. They would be back, bigger and brasher than ever.

# 1959

## GET THAT CHEVY FEELING...FAST!

Chevrolet approached the end of the decade with completely restyled cars that had grown longer and wider yet again. Compared to the 1958 models, the '59 offerings had a 1.5in-longer wheelbase and were more than 2in wider (only 0.1in narrower than a '59 Cadillac!), but at the same time, the roofline sat an inch closer to the ground. The contrast was incredible.

Even more incredible was the dramatic rear-end styling. Fins were back, but instead of soaring vertically, as on Cadillacs, Chevys had huge, horizontal, spreading gull wings, unlike any other make. Below the razor-sharp edges of the fins, two giant teardrop taillights dominated the back panel. Jim Whipple, of *Car Life*, had this to say: "...the man who says that he wasn't just a bit bug-eyed when he first saw that gull-wing rear deck is either too blasé or an outright liar." Equally startling was the new front-end look, which featured two enormous "eyebrows" set in the leading edge of the hood.

**Dramatic styling changes abounded in 1959, as Chevys like this sport coupe became even longer, wider and lower. Huge "eyebrow" slots in the leading edge of the hood were an innovation, but the grille teeth seem like a retrograde step. The two-door hardtop has wonderful all-round visibility, thanks to slim roof pillars, and is an excellent example of "a convertible with a steel roof".**

Industry observers commented that the increase in dimensions represented a move by Chevrolet away from the low-price market to the medium-price bracket. Undoubtedly, this was true, and the culmination of a trend that had developed gradually over the previous three years. The 1959 Chevys used the same basic Fisher B-body as Pontiac, Oldsmobile and Buick, instead of the smaller A-body they had previously only shared with Pontiac at the bottom of the GM ladder. "The day of the 'little Chevy' has passed," wrote Al Berger in *Speed Age*, adding "...the 1959 Chevrolet is a spectacular car. It's big, clean lined and radically styled, with all the passenger and luggage space, and performance the car owner could want." In those far-off days, it was accepted, almost unanimously, that bigger was better, and Chevrolet aimed to provide a car of the same size as a Cadillac or Lincoln, but at half the price.

Practically the only complaints voiced about the bigger Chevy concerned the low level of the seats and the difficulty experienced by rear-seat passengers when getting in and out, even with four-door models. Otherwise, it was praise all the way, the trunk capacity being compared to that of a pre-war pick-up truck. The advice given to people who couldn't fit three across the vast

*Above* **There was no central hood ornament in 1959, just the crossed flags and Chevrolet name in script on the leading edge, between the "eyebrows".**

*Right* **Without doubt, the most spectacular feature of the '59 Chevy is the gull-wing rear, the almost horizontal fins sweeping gracefully outward to razor-like edges. The giant teardrop rear lights are equally bold. Apart from the styling, one benefit provided by this design is the huge trunk space: "...just about the most capacious in history," stated one observer. It has been said that the fins act as wings and actually cause the rear of the car to lift at speeds over 100mph, but this seems unlikely. The fuel filler cap is hidden behind the hinged license plate. Note the dummy air inlet at the rear of the roof, a styling feature carried over from 1958.**

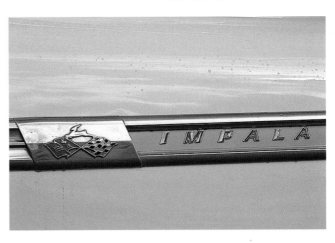

*Above* **With all the raindrops around it, and a gaping mouth, one of the front fender ornaments looks like a cross between a jet aircraft and a fish - a "jetfish"?**

*Above* **The Impala identification, with its crossed flags and leaping antelope, is carried in the middle of the side body trim.**

*Above*  While the front seat backs fold forward to give access to the rear seat, the low roof and low seat squab make climbing in or out of the car an awkward exercise. There isn't much legroom in the back either. Front-seat occupants have to beware of banging their knees on the edge of the windshield frame as they get in and out.

*Above*  Set in the rear seat, the recessed radio speaker carries the crossed flags and leaping antelope motif.

*Below*  Although the roofline sweeps elegantly down to the trunk, it does produce problems for rear-seat passengers: even with four-door models, people find difficulty when getting in and out of the car.

bench seat was to go on a diet! The reduction in height was Harley Earl's doing, of course, but by now even he realized that his cars had reached the limit that would be tolerated by drivers and passengers of average agility.

For a car approaching 20ft in length, and tipping the scales at well over a ton and a half, the '59 Chevy was no sluggard, especially if equipped with the 315hp Special Super Turbo-Thrust 348cu.in V8 with 11.0:1 compression and three two-barrel carburetors. Even in standard form, with a single four-barrel and 9.5:1 compression ratio, the 348 engine produced 250hp, enough to hustle the Impala to 60mph in about 10sec, or less, and on to a top speed of around 123mph. Mind you, there were rumors that at speeds above 100mph, those big back wings generated enough lift to cause instability. Whether this story has any basis in fact, or is simply another piece of Chevrolet folklore, is difficult to say.

What is far easier to determine is that Chevy branched out into a distinct new automotive market area in 1959 with the El Camino. Two years earlier, Ford had debuted their Ranchero, and had outsold Chevrolet's truck-based Cameo in the burgeoning leisure vehicle sector by a ratio of almost ten to one. It had taken time for Chevy to catch up. However, having decided to compete, the "bow-tie boys" certainly came up with a winner. Built with the same "Vista-top" lines as the passenger cars, the El Camino was actually based on the bottom-of-the-line Biscayne Brookwood station wagon, and came with an interior trimmed in the same manner. In addition to the gull-wings and everything else, the El Camino had a wraparound rear window beneath the cantilevered trailing edge of the flat roof, as was found on the hardtop sedans.

The El Camino came in two models: the 1180, with a 235.5cu.in six-cylinder engine, and the 1280, which was fitted with a 283cu.in V8. However, there was the usual comprehensive options list, which included everything

*Above* **The driver is faced by a group of round, hooded instruments, the five-circle theme being repeated in the steering wheel. The speedometer dominates the dash, but the overall presentation is clean and uncluttered. An electric clock, on the right, was standard on Impalas, but optional on cheaper Bel Airs and Biscaynes.**

---

**1959 CHEVROLET IMPALA
TWO-DOOR SPORT COUPE**

**Engine:**
OHV V8, cast-iron block and heads
Capacity: 348cu.in (5.70 liters)
Bore and stroke: 4.125x3.25in
Compression ratio: 9.5:1
Power output: 250hp at 4,400rpm
Torque: 355lb/ft at 2,800 rpm
Carburetor: Single four-barrel

**Transmission:**
Three-speed manual

**Chassis/body:**
Wheelbase: 119in
Overall length: 210.9in
Overall width: 79.9in
Overall height: 56in
Shipping weight: 3,580lb
Suspension: Coil springs all round; independent front and live axle rear
Wheel diameter: 14in

**Performance:**
Top speed: 123mph
0-60mph: 10.7sec
Standing quarter mile: 18.5sec at 80mph

**General:**
Factory price, 1959: $2,717
Production total: 164,901*

*Total number of 1959 Chevrolet two-door sport coupes built; no separate figures for Impala series available.

up to the high-performance 348cu.in big-block engine. Sales were encouraging, slightly over 20,000 units finding buyers, which was far better than the Cameo had ever done. One of the reasons for the El Camino's success was the fact that it drove like a car, but still had a useful carrying capacity, even if the load space was restricted by those great big wings.

In the passenger-car catalog, the Del Ray name had been replaced by Biscayne for the base models. The Bel Air became the middle-priced series, while the top-of-the-line cars (which included the only Chevy convertible) were called Impalas. The proliferation of engine choice, which was to become the norm in the 1960s, was just beginning to be seen in 1959, when eight different specifications were available. These ranged from the mundane 135hp, 235.5cu.in six to the aforementioned hot 348. In between, with four levels of tune on offer, was the ever popular 283cu.in V8.

The 283 was still the only powerplant offered in the Corvette, the 290hp, fuel injected version giving Chevy's sports car performance figures of 0-60mph in 6.6sec, 0-100mph in 15.5sec, and a maximum speed of 128mph. The cost of such exhilaration didn't come cheap, however: the engine option alone added $484 to the price, and by the time you tacked on a four-speed manual transmission with floor shift ($188), heavy-duty brakes and suspension ($425), and a Positraction rear axle ($48), the check was increased by more than a grand. And if you wanted such luxury items as a power top, transistor radio, DeLuxe heater and so on, the eventual price tag for your new 'Vette could be almost 50 percent higher than the advertised factory figure.

The same principle applied to the full-sized Chevy automobiles and trucks. Indeed, even basic items, such as an oil filter ($9), which inevitably would be included in any customer's requirements, were listed as optional extras. Performance apart, in appearance, the 1959 Corvettes were little different from those of the previous year, although designer Bill Mitchell had attempted to clean up the lines by deleting the fake hood louvers and the chrome strips on the trunk lid.

Chevy trucks remained much as before, too, most of the Massive-Functional styling of 1958 being retained. Only the hood and front fender emblems were revised. Due to the recession, greater emphasis was placed on fuel economy in commercial vehicles, and Chevy intro-

*Above* **This assembly-line photo shows an Impala four-door sport sedan body being dropped onto its chassis. Note the "flat-top" roofline, which differs from the sloping style used on the standard sedans and coupes.**

*Above right* **Nearing the end of the assembly line. Batteries, windshield wipers and hub caps are almost the last items to be installed. It is also at this stage that the lights and turn signals of each vehicle are tested. The car nearest the camera is a Bel Air four-door sedan, while on the far left, you can just make out the Chevy truck production line.**

*Right* **What do you put on the back of your sales brochure? Why, a rear view of the car, of course! And when it's a 1959 Chevrolet Impala four-door sport sedan hardtop, with huge areas of panoramic glass, gull-wing rear deck and giant teardrop lights, what more could you possibly need?**

duced a new camshaft for its Thriftmaster six that was said to boost mpg by up to ten percent. Otherwise, most of the promotion centered around the Flight-Ride cab with its Panoramic windshield, High-Level ventilation and Nu-Flex seats. A Custom Cab package added extra chrome, arm rests, sun visors and a cigarette lighter.

Chevrolet achieved increased vehicle production in 1959, despite a 116-day strike by the United Steel Workers of America, which began in mid-July. On November 7, the Taft-Hartley Act was invoked, and the resulting 80-day injunction issued by the US Supreme Court set the steel mills rolling once again, but for a period there was a critical shortage of steel components, and during November, many Chevy assembly plants were either shut down or operating at a fraction of their normal output. This handicap allowed Ford to catch up, and the two giants of Detroit entered the next decade running almost neck and neck, with Chevy ahead by a whisker. But, with one or two exceptions, the 1950s had belonged to Chevrolet, and the company more than deserved the accolade of America's number one.

*Above* **The fake hood louvers have gone, so has some of the chrome, but otherwise a 1959 Corvette looks exactly like a '58. The main change came in increased performance, but that didn't come cheap: it was easy to bump the price of a new '59 'Vette by as much as 50 percent if you went for all the hot options.**

*Above right* **New for 1959 was the El Camino, which doubled as personal transportation and, with a carrying capacity of 1,150lb, practical load hauler. Combining passenger-car styling, comfort and handling with truck utility, the El Camino reached a first-year production figure of 22,246 units. It was based on the Biscayne Brookwood station wagon, with Bel Air body trim, and the wraparound rear window and cantilevered roof of the hardtop sport sedan, making it a stylish package.**

*Right* **The only changes to Chevy trucks for 1959 were revised hood and front fender emblems. This Apache Series 32 step-side pick-up has the standard cab with a small rear window, and there's virtually no chrome anywhere - very much how a working truck would have left the factory.**

# CHEVROLETS FOR SHOW 'N' GO

It should come as no surprise that Chevrolets have always been popular candidates for racing and modifying. As America's number-one car producer, Chevy could provide much more material for the hot rodder, customizer and racer to play with, and there has never been any shortage of "bow-tie enthusiasts" to take advantage of that fact. But it was the arrival of Chevy's 265cu.in small-block V8, in 1955, that really struck the spark and fanned it into flames, giving Chevrolet the image of performance at an affordable price.

Most popular, of course, are the 1955, 1956 and 1957 Chevys. No other 1950s car has created the enormous following that these Chevrolets enjoy. Be it on the drag strip, at a custom car show, or in a classic concours d'elegance, a healthy display of these Chevys will always be in attendance, drawing the crowds. This is true around the world: in Europe, Scandinavia and Australia, just as in their homeland, the '55-'57 Chevys are tops.

But wherever there are 1950s Chevrolets, there are red-blooded car people who enjoy nothing more than taking these mass produced automobiles and trucks, and turning them into something extra special.

**Ron Harding Jr lays down a tremendous burn-out in his Super Comp '57 Chevy during the 1991 NHRA Winston World Finals at Pomona, California.**

*Above* **The exquisite "Spirit of '57" drag racing Corvette even has the two small dummy air scoops on the front fenders of what is, undoubtedly, a replica bodyshell. Note the airbrushed front grille.**

*Below* **The desert storming '55 Chevy of Larry Schwacofer leaps a hill during the 1985 Mint 400 off-road race, staged in the wastelands outside the gambling mecca of Las Vegas, Nevada.**

*Above* **This brilliant yellow custom '50 Chevy DeLuxe two-door coupe features a 4in roof chop, is radically lowered all around, and has a '53 Chevy grille with extra teeth. Owner Marlyn Englert, from Minneapolis, Minnesota, used a Camaro front clip and Nova rear end to modernize the Chevy's ride, but stuck with a trusty 250cu.in Stovebolt six for vintage motorvation.**

*Right* **A Chevy inline-six might not be most people's choice for an engine, but thanks to speed equipment from specialists like Clifford and Sissel, plus a healthy dose of nitrous oxide, this custom '50 Chevy moves out with the best of them.**

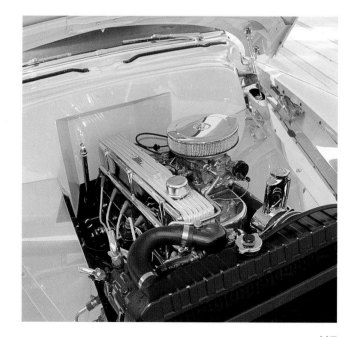

*Right* **A classic example of a "kustom kemp" is this '58 Impala. A chrome tube front grille, scalloped paint, side pipes and Appleton spotlights all help provide the 1950s look. This is enhanced by a radical lowering job (6in at the front and 5in at the rear). Kool, man!**

*Below* **This mild custom '54 Chevy Bel Air features extra teeth in the grille, a smoothed-out appearance achieved by removing all the badges and emblems, and Appletons. Its ground hugging appearance was obtained by cutting the front coil springs and relocating the spindles, and by de-arching the rear springs and installing 4in lowering blocks. Don't it look neat?**

*Below right* **This '55 Chevy hot rod is more at home on the drag strip than cruising to the local burger joint. It has had a long life as a racer, both in the US and in Europe, where it now resides. Power comes from a reworked 396cu.in Chevy big-block V8.**

*Above* Lowered, custom wheels, a late-model front clip, and a healthy supercharged small-block Chevy V8 - the perfect recipe for a smart looking and good driving pick-up. This white '52 half-ton truck is superb.

*Right* When boat builder Jim Bryant, of Knoxville, Tennessee, put together this fiberglass-bodied 1957 Chevrolet for Rob Vandergriff to drive, he didn't know that it was going to be one of the most influential drag racing cars constructed in recent years. The combination of a huge 1,000+hp, 600cu.in V8, loads of nitrous oxide, and a '57 Chevy body, running close to 200mph in 6sec, was to spawn a whole new class of these wild machines in the Pro Modified category.

*Below right* Early 1950s Chevy fastback models also respond well to the customizer's art. This superb example belongs to guitarist Jimmy Vaughn.

*Below* The rear fins of this custom convertible have been altered so much that few people would recognize it as a '54 Chevrolet.

# CHEVROLET PRODUCTION FOR THE 1950s

The table shown below sets out the number of vehicles built in the USA by Chevrolet throughout the 1950s. Unless otherwise noted, the figures relate to model year production, not the calendar year. While these figures have been cross-referenced and verified wherever possible, different sources of this information often tend to give quite widely varying numbers, so unfortunately no guarantee as to the absolute accuracy of the totals can be given.

|      | Automobiles | Light-duty trucks | Corvette |
|------|-------------|-------------------|----------|
| 1950 | 1,498,590   | 368,184*          |          |
| 1951 | 1,229,986   | 291,834*          |          |
| 1952 | 818,142     | 272,249**         |          |
| 1953 | 1,346,475   | 274,759*          | 300      |
| 1954 | 1,143,561   | 235,423*          | 3,640    |
| 1955 | 1,704,667   | 284,394*          | 700      |
| 1956 | 1,567,117   | 253,197*          | 3,467    |
| 1957 | 1,505,910   | 254,113*          | 6,339    |
| 1958 | 1,142,460   | 204,221*          | 9,168    |
| 1959 | 1,462,140   | 245,873*          | 9,670    |

* Calendar year figure.

** Calendar year figure for all Chevrolet commercial vehicles, no breakdown for light-duty trucks (under 10,000lb GVW) is available.

## CHEVROLET OVERSEAS

Although often overlooked today, in the 1950s, Chevrolet, and General Motors as a whole, were much more interested in exporting vehicles than they have been until relatively recently. Unquestionably, it was a profitable enterprise for them, with thousands of vehicles shipped around the world each year.

Exports were the responsibility of General Motors Overseas Operations, based in New York City which, in the 1960s, became General Motors Overseas Distribution Corporation. GMOO dictated which models were to be exported or assembled overseas, leaving Chevrolet Engineering to create the vehicles with the appropriate modifications, such as right-hand drive.

There were two main methods of sending autos abroad - ready built cars were known as Single-Unit Packs (SUP), while kits of parts requiring assembly were called either Completely Knocked Down (CKD) or Semi Knocked Down (SKD). SKD kits were complete cars, while CKD kits needed certain components to be supplied in the country of destination.

The production of CKD kits dates back to the 1920s. In 1928 (the peak year for exports), GM shipped approximately 290,000 vehicles abroad, a healthy percentage of them being Chevrolets. By 1962, nearly 90 percent of GM vehicles sold outside the USA and Canada were made in the foreign countries where they were to be marketed, and at the end of the 1969 model year, right-hand-drive CKD production ceased, and thereafter only left-hand-drive CKD kits were put together, mainly for the Mexican and South African plants.

The European market was generally supplied with SUP cars that needed only a small amount of final assembly work to ready them for sale. Usually, cars intended for use by US and Canadian embassies were also SUP versions, but in commercial terms these vehicles had some drawbacks, as they provided little scope for the receiving country to benefit from manufacturing, apart from any extras they added. Sometimes, this caused heavy import taxes to be levied, and SUP cars were often the subject of quotas restricting the number of vehicles allowed into a particular country.

However, CKD cars were looked on more favorably for the economic opportunities they offered by requiring both locally made parts and labor to build them. CKD vehicles comprised mainly mechanical and body parts, with items like glass, tires, interior trim and final paint-work still needed to finish them off. Other alterations, such as additional or special lighting and right-hand-drive conversions, were also carried out locally; some-times even wiring harnesses were added at this stage.

Assembly of CKD kits varied from country to country, depending on GMOO's policy. In some years in Aus-tralia and New Zealand, for example, only one Chevy model would be built, while in South Africa, a range of cars could be offered. In South Africa, all kits were US sourced up to 1956, then there was a mixture of Canadian and US supply until the 1958 and later model years, which were totally Canadian in origin.

Furthermore, some overseas assembly plants not only built cars for domestic consumption, but also shipped them to other countries. GM Continental in Antwerp, Belgium, supplied various European nations, including the UK, and right-hand-drive markets in Southern Africa. GM Suisse exported to Italy and Austria; while GM Inter-national in Copenhagen, Denmark, and GM Nordska, Stockholm, Sweden, supplied Scandinavia.

GM South Africa appears to have exported some cars to Australia (as well as other African nations), as con-cessions were given to vehicles traveling between British Commonwealth countries under the Common-wealth Preference scheme. In the UK, the McKenna Duties put a 33 percent tax on imported automobiles, and this was later extended to include imported car parts as well. This level of duty lasted into the 1960s, then it was gradually reduced.

Of course, GM also exported cars to Canada.

*Below* **'57 Chevrolets nearing the end of the assembly line, at the head of the queue is a One-Fifty Handyman two-door station wagon.**

Corvettes were only ever built in the USA, and depending on the year, other models not built in Canada (such as station wagons and the El Camino) were imported too. Few, if any, Canadian Chevrolets were exported to the USA in the 1950s, as before the "Auto Pact" between the two countries, normal import tariffs were applied to vehicles crossing the border. Canadian built Chevy trucks were sold under the Maple Leaf brand.

In Australia, GM bought Holden's Motor Body Builders of Adelaide in 1931 and reorganized the company as General Motors Holden's Pty Ltd, which engaged in manufacturing components and assembling CKD cars from both the USA and Canada. During World War 2, GM decided to manufacture cars in Australia in addition to the assembly-only operations, and this production commenced in 1948. In an attempt to encourage and develop their own auto industry, Australia only allowed one SUP car to be imported for every four CKD cars.

Obtaining production data from all the countries where GM had factories assembling Chevrolets from CKD kits, over 40 years ago, is almost impossible because records have either been accidentally destroyed (by fire and flood), which happened in South Africa, or deliberately thrown away, as at GM-Holden in Australia. In

such cases, the researcher's only recourse is to use body numbers, Vehicle Identification Numbers (VIN) and annual registration figures. The problem with this last method is that as yearly registration totals are inclusive of any Chevrolet first registered between January 1 and December 31, they do not differentiate between used imports (and there were a few), complete new cars from the USA or Canada, and locally assembled models.

To complicate matters further, in Australia at least, from 1949 onwards, all new models of locally assembled Chevrolets were generally first released between April and June, depending on the continuity of component shipments. Therefore, a calendar-year registration figure would contain a proportion of cars from a different model year. As can be imagined, it usually took some time for the foreign plants to prepare new tooling, hence the delay in introducing new models.

Chevrolets for overseas markets were manufactured either in Canada, at the Oshawa, Ontario plant, or at the Tarrytown, New York factory, although some bodies (station wagons, for example) were apparently built elsewhere. Chevrolet engines produced at the Flint, Michigan or Tonawanda, New York plants were routinely sent to the Oshawa factory for use in both domestic and export models, or occasionally shipped directly to the country in question. Engines from the Oshawa and Windsor, Ontario plants were also exported.

Some may not consider the CKD cars to be "proper" Chevrolets, but without this form of assembly, it's unlikely that Chevy would have become so established in overseas markets. The one thing Chevrolet automobiles did in the 1950s, wherever they were sold, was to provide a glamor and status that were often not offered by local manufacturers.

*Left* **The body of a 1958 Impala two-door coupe is dropped onto its chassis.**

*Right* **Corvettes have only ever been manufactured in the USA. Here, a 1958 'Vette body is about to be mated to its chassis on the St Louis, Missouri production line.**

## OVERSEAS CKD KIT PRODUCTION

| | GM Continental | GM Suisse | GM-Holden* |
|---|---|---|---|
| | Belgium | Switzerland | Australia |
| 1950 | 6,271 | 1,358 | 1,454 |
| 1951 | 7,811 | 1,944 | 1,789 |
| 1952 | 6,273 | 1,007 | 1,418 |
| 1953 | 6,264 | 1,368 | 2,052 |
| 1954 | 6,691 | 1,225 | 1,519 |
| 1955 | 8,469 | 1,488 | 2,055 |
| 1956 | 7,152 | 1,176 | 1,346 |
| 1957 | 4,015 | 884 | 1,861 |
| 1958 | 3,583 | 629 | 1,152** |
| 1959 | 3,030 | 689 | 1,911 |

*Note* Figures shown for Belgium and Switzerland are for cars only; no commercial vehicles are included.

* Estimated production figures for four-door sedans only; excludes coupe utility models and commercial vehicles.

** Correct total of 1958 four-door sedans assembled.

## CHEVROLET OF CANADA PRODUCTION

(Source: *Ward's Canadian Automotive Yearbook*)

| | Automobiles | Trucks |
|---|---|---|
| 1950 | 61,147 | 24,571* |
| 1951 | 81,908 | 34,041* |
| 1952 | 85,110 | 39,396* |
| 1953 | 95,639 | 36,038* |
| 1954 | 54,286 | 22,026* |
| 1955 | 62,819 | 17,125 |
| 1956 | 70,236 | 22,827 |
| 1957 | 76,353 | 16,523 |
| 1958 | 73,382 | 15,997 |
| 1959 | 69,578 | 16,970 |

* Includes military truck production.

## GM OVERSEAS ASSEMBLY PLANTS

Argentina - Buenos Aires

Australia -

Manufacturing plants: Fishermans Bend, Melbourne, Victoria; Woodville, Adelaide, South Australia

Assembly plants: Acica Ridge, Brisbane, Queensland; Dandenong, Melbourne, Victoria; Elizabeth, Adelaide, South Australia; Pagewood, Sydney, New South Wales; Perth, Western Australia

Belgium - Antwerp

Brazil - Sao Caetano, Sao Paulo

Canada - Oshawa, Ontario

Chile - Santiago

Cuba - Havana

Denmark - Copenhagen

India - Bombay (to 1950)

Mexico - Mexico City

New Zealand - Petone, Wellington

Peru - Lima

South Africa - Port Elizabeth

Sweden - Stockholm (to 1956 model year)

Switzerland - Biel

Uruguay - Montevideo (still to be confirmed)

Venezuela - Caracas

# ACKNOWLEDGMENTS

Firstly, and most importantly, my extreme gratitude goes to photographer Mike Key and his wife, June. Mike is responsible for the vast majority of the pictures in this book, and without his expertise, tremendous energy, enthusiasm and willingness to help, plus June's unfailing good humor throughout, it would have been impossible for me to complete this project.

I would also like to thank the following people who made invaluable contributions:

Ruth Bouldes and Melissa Garman at Chevrolet Public Relations, Warren, Michigan.

Paul Hilton of Newbury, Berkshire, and David Hayward of Southampton, Hampshire, UK, for overseas sales information; Peter Kelly of Ivanhoe, Victoria, Australia for providing Australian data; Tom Tytor of the National Library of Canada, Ottawa, Canada.

All the owners of the vehicles featured, in particular: Tony Ellis of Brixworth, Northampton, UK (1950); Phil Townend from Wraysbury, Middlesex, UK (1951); Paul Wells, Edgware, Middlesex, UK (1952); Tom Garvin, boss man at Touch of Glass, Le Seur, Minnesota (1953);

Glen Hardwick of Grays, Essex, UK (1954); Derald and Nola DeVries, Forreston, Illinois (1955); Don and Pat Wheeler, Aurora, Missouri (1956); Phil and Sallie Miller, Little Rock, Arkansas (1957); Nick Howson from Harwich, Essex, UK (1958); Stephen Morgan of Parkstone, Dorset, UK (1959). And all the other owners for providing us with such a glittering array of 1950s Chevrolets.

Thanks also to Bryan Kennedy for starting the ball rolling; Ian Penberthy; Clive Househam of CHPublications; John and Ian Dowdeswell of Brooklands Books; Peter Robain; Mike Hodges; and Ray Groves of Corvette Kingdom.

Finally, special thanks must go to my wife Jennie and son John, who have constantly supported me over the years and boosted my spirits whenever the going got tough or deadlines were looming.

*Tony Beadle*

*London*

*January 1997*

**PHOTO CREDITS**
All of the photographs in this book are by Mike Key, with the exception of the following:
Tony Beadle: pp. 1, 8, 9, 10, 11 bottom, 12 bottom, 13, 14 top, 15, 16, 18, 19 top, 41, 50 bottom, 54 top, 59 top, 69 top, 111 bottom, 112, 113 bottom, 114/115, 116 top; Chevrolet/GM Photographic: pp. 11 top, 14 bottom, 17, 20 bottom, 33, 40 bottom, 44 top, 51 bottom, 54 bottom, 59 bottom, 66, 67 bottom, 77, 88, 97, 110, 111 top, 113 top, 123, 124, 125; Indianapolis Motor Speedway: pp. 12, 67 top; Peter Robain: pp. 28/29, 30 bottom, 128; BFGoodrich Tire Co: p. 116 bottom.

# BIBLIOGRAPHY

Cast Iron Wonder by Doug Bell (Clymer Publications, 1961)

Chevrolet 1955 - Creating The Original by Michael Lamm (Lamm Morada Inc, 1991)

Chevrolet 1955-1957 (Brooklands Books)

Chevrolet 1955-1957 (Publications International Ltd, 1987)

Chevrolet Corvette by Philip Bingham (Salamander Books Ltd, 1990)

Chevrolet Corvette Gold Portfolio 1953-1962 (Brooklands Books)

Chevrolet Impala and SS (Brooklands Books)

Chevrolet Pickups 1946-1972 by John Gunnell (Motorbooks International, 1988)

Chevy El Camino and SS (Brooklands Books)

Corvette Roadster (Publications International Ltd, 1986)

Corvette! Thirty Years of Great Advertising, Edited by William Clark (Princeton Publishing Inc, 1983)

Early Chevrolet Corvettes by Thomas Falconer (Osprey, 1985)

Encyclopedia of American Cars 1930-1980 by Richard Langworth (Publications International Ltd, 1984)

Harley Earl by Stephen Bayley (Trefoil Publications Ltd, 1990)

Illustrated Chevrolet Buyer's Guide by John Gunnell (Motorbooks International, 1989)

My Years With General Motors by Alfred P. Sloan (Sidgwick & Jackson Ltd, 1986)

Standard Catalog of American Cars 1805-1942, Edited by Beverly Rae Kimes and Henry Austin Clark Jr (Krause Publications, 1985)

Standard Catalog of American Cars 1946-1975, Edited by John Gunnell (Krause Publications, 1987)

Standard Catalog of American Light-Duty Trucks, Edited by John Gunnell (Krause Publications, 1993)

The Corvettes by Richard Langworth (Motor Racing Publications Ltd, 1988)

The Heavyweight Book of American Light Trucks 1939-1966 by Tom Brownell and Don Bunn (Motorbooks International, 1988)

# THE AUTHOR

Freelance writer and photographer Tony Beadle is, among other things, editor of *Triumph World* magazine, a top-quality, bi-monthly publication devoted to the cars produced by the British manufacturer Standard-Triumph, which has gained a huge international following since its launch in 1995. He is also associate editor of *Street Machine*, a monthly magazine that deals with hot rods and custom cars. He was the founder editor of *Classic American* magazine, and has also edited *American Car World* magazine.

Regarded as one of Britain's foremost authorities on the American automobile, and an avid lover of classic Americana, Tony bought his first US car - a 1949 Ford V8 Custom four-door sedan that cost less than $50 - in 1964, and has driven Detroit steel almost exclusively ever since. In a country where gasoline is an expensive commodity and cars travel on the left-hand side of the road, this preference for large automobiles with V8 engines and the steering wheel on the "wrong" side is regarded as slightly eccentric by some.

Over the years, he has owned or driven every modern make of American car, but has a particular affection for the lesser known marques, especially American Motors Corporation, Rambler, Studebaker and Crosley. Yet to fulfill a long held ambition to possess a 1956 Cadillac convertible, Tony currently has a 1968 AMC Javelin in his garage that is being prepared for drag racing.

*Chevrolets of the 1950s* is Tony's third book about American vehicles, and he has several more automotive books in the pipeline.